EARTH MAGICK

First published in 2022 by Leaping Hare Press
an imprint of The Quarto Group.
The Old Brewery, 6 Blundell Street
London, N7 9BH,
United Kingdom
T (0)20 7700 6700
www.Quarto.com

A catalog record for this book is available from the British Library.

ISBN 978-0-7112-7172-2
Ebook ISBN 978-0-7112-7173-9

10 9 8 7 6 5 4 3 2 1

Commissioning editor Chloe Murphy
Cover & interior illustrations by Viki Lester of Forensics & Flowers
Design by Georgina Hewitt

Printed in China

The publisher would like to thank the following for permission
to reproduce copyright material:

Shutterstock/ marina_ua

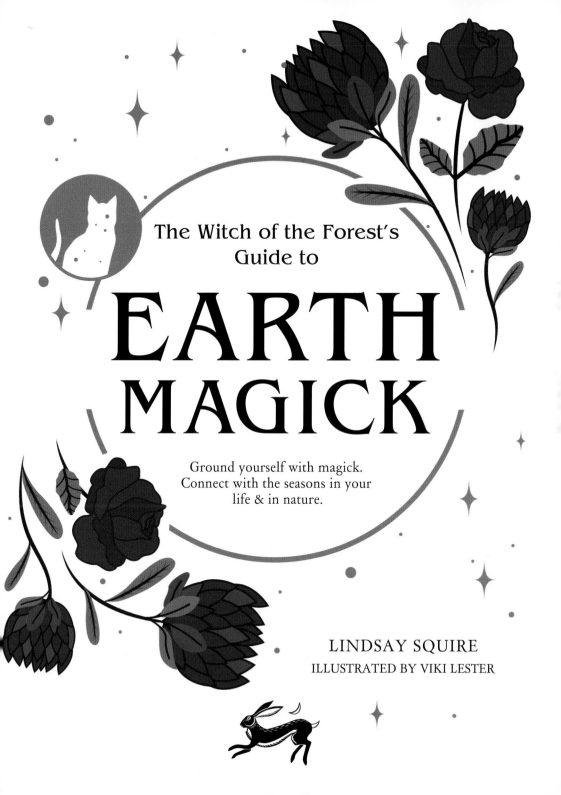

The Witch of the Forest's
Guide to

EARTH
MAGICK

Ground yourself with magick.
Connect with the seasons in your
life & in nature.

LINDSAY SQUIRE

ILLUSTRATED BY VIKI LESTER

CONTENTS

MY STORY

The woods and forests around my childhood home played a large part in shaping my Craft before I was even conscious of it.

From a young age, I felt a strong pull toward nature and the Earth, and I spent many a Sunday morning walking through the forests with my dad. I would always come back home with my pockets full of items I'd found along the way— feathers, leaves, and flowers to put in my press, a rock or two that I felt compelled to pick up and bring home with me, and seasonal goodies like conkers and chestnuts. It's funny to see how things haven't really changed—after a walk in the forest, I still come home with all kinds of foraged natural gifts!

Magick is a wonderful form of nourishment that helps us to connect to the energies of the Earth around us, and can teach us how to connect with our own energies on a deeper level. As you discover more about the Craft, you discover so much about yourself. When I began my Witchcraft journey over a decade ago, I was practicing in secret, or "in the broom closet."

While I was in the broom closet, my connection to the Earth was incredibly important. Simply walking through the forest near where I was living at the time or walking barefoot in the yard became deep and meaningful rituals.

I was unable to practice my Craft as I wanted to in many ways, but I was able to nurture my connection to the natural world and this strengthened my connection to the Earth. It's this connection and relationship that has helped to inspire this and my first book, *Natural Magick*. My hope is that together, these books will equip you not only with knowledge of the basic principles of Witchcraft, but will give you the confidence to incorporate them into your own practice, and use them to deepen your connection with the natural world.

Wherever you are on your own path, I hope this book helps you along.

I am truly honored that I am able to continue to walk with you on your path as you have walked with me on mine.

Lindsay

THINGS TO KNOW BEFORE
you embark on your journey through this book:

Your energy is the most important tool for growth

Everything is made of energy, from the ground beneath our feet to the rest of the natural world around us. We all have our own inner energy, which is essential to practicing Witchcraft. Learning how to control it allows us to have control of our mind, body, and spirit. Although it could take a while, learning to master this will help to transform your Witchcraft journey and help you grow on a personal level. All you need is your energy and a willingness to learn.

Caring for your energy is a vital part of Witchcraft

The book focuses on how connecting with the energies of the Earth can help us to better understand and connect with our own personal energy. Caring for our own energy is a vital part of Witchcraft, as it is our personal energy that drives our Craft and determines the effectiveness of our practice. Learning to care for your energy is a vital form of self-care, as your energy is the most important tool you need for growth and transformation on your Witchcraft journey.

Facing your light and dark energy will strengthen your practice

Confronting your shadows and the feelings and thoughts you've been trying to ignore can act as a springboard for getting to know and understand yourself on a deeper level. This is not only important for your personal growth and development, but it enriches your Witchcraft practice, too. While it doesn't promise to be an easy journey, it will be a very worthwhile one! Better understanding of your dark side will strengthen your sense of intuition. It will help you better identify who you are as a Witch and the path that feels right for you.

We all have our own unique seasons and energy

We all experience unique ebbs and flows of energy. Sometimes, our energy doesn't always sync with the seasons of the natural world, the cycles of the Moon, or the Sabbats. It doesn't mean that you don't have a good connection to the Moon or nature, or that you are any less of a Witch for feeling this way—all it shows is that we have our own energetic cycles, and this gives you an opportunity to connect with your own energy, and better understand what you need at that time.

You don't have to flourish all year round

The world is a busy place, and we can get swept along with it, where we are constantly expected to give our all 365 days a year. But like the natural world, it's ok to pause to take a rest if your energy is low. We have four seasons so that nature is able to rest and restore herself after the life and growth of spring and summer. Following Mother Nature's lead, taking regular time to rest so we can recharge and renew our energies is very healthy, not only for your body, but your mind and spirit too.

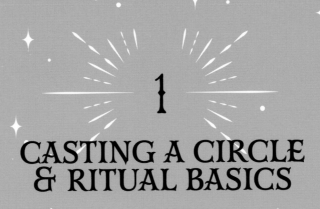

1
CASTING A CIRCLE
& RITUAL BASICS

When it comes to casting spells or performing a ritual, there are a few basics to think about before you begin. Practices such as casting a circle and calling the elements can help to concentrate the energy you raise with your magickal workings.

It's important to note that not all magickal traditions make use of a circle or call upon the elements. It can depend on which branch of witchcraft you follow. If you don't follow a particular tradition, it's up to you to decide whether they feel right and appropriate to you. In this chapter, I'll share ways to cast a circle and call the elements, as well as the theories behind them, so you have enough information to decide whether these practices are ones you wish to adopt yourself.

Spell after-care is also very important, and looking after yourself and your energy is crucial. You can feel drained after a spell or ritual, so it's good to know what to do to restore this energy and achieve a sense of equilibrium. Over time, you'll begin to see which techniques work better and which don't. It's important to do what feels right to you and understand what recharges your energy.

WITCHCRAFT
& Ethics

The practice of Witchcraft itself as a spiritual path isn't governed by a one-size-fits-all moral code or specific set of beliefs. There are many different branches and traditions of Witchcraft, each with their own practices and ethics.

I think it's important for you to start to figure out where you fit in terms of ethics before you begin casting spells or performing rituals. Will you follow the ethics of a particular branch of Witchcraft, letting that be your guide, or will you follow your own moral code based on what does and doesn't feel right, regardless of tradition? There is no right or wrong answer, just the way that feels right to you.

THREE-FOLD LAW AND THE WICCAN REDE

Wiccans believe in the Three-Fold Law and the Rede. The Three-Fold Law is simple: whatever you send out into the universe, be it negative or positive, will come back to you three-fold. If you use your magick for any negative purpose, eventually the negative energy sent out will somehow return to you and have a negative impact on your life. The Three-Fold Law is part of the Wiccan Rede, which is the key moral system for practicing magick for Wiccans and some Neopagans. The Rede states "An it harm none, do what thou will." It asks Wiccans to think about

the consequences of their actions and not to purposely cause harm to others through magick and mundane means.

OTHER MORAL CODES

There are other branches of Witchcraft that don't follow the Rede or the Three-Fold Law. Personally, I don't hold to the Rede. When I practiced Wicca many years ago, it was always a focus of contention for me, and it was one of the reasons why I found myself drifting toward traditional and then latterly, eclectic Witchcraft. It's not that I want to use my magick to cause harm to others, but basing my Craft on my own moral code feels more comfortable to me than having a rule to follow. This comes from my Christian background where, for years, I had to be seen to follow the very rigid rules of the church while practicing "in the broom closet."

When it came to my practice of Witchcraft, I wanted to follow my own intuition and sense of right and wrong. Basing my Craft on my own moral code gave me a spiritual freedom I hadn't experienced for years and put me in full control of the direction my spiritual path was taking.

Find your own way. Some witches believe in karma, which is very similar to the Three-Fold Law. This holds that what you send out comes back to you eventually. If this is your belief, honor it and do what feels authentic to you.

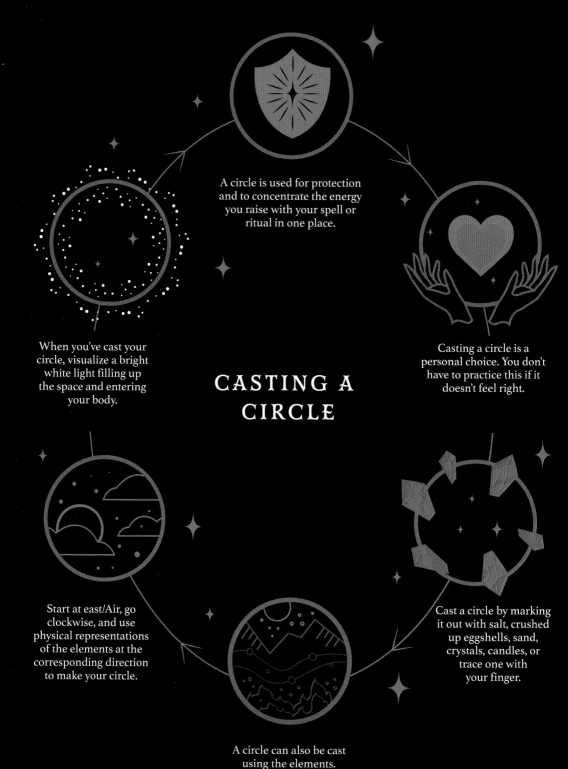

A circle is used for protection and to concentrate the energy you raise with your spell or ritual in one place.

Casting a circle is a personal choice. You don't have to practice this if it doesn't feel right.

CASTING A CIRCLE

When you've cast your circle, visualize a bright white light filling up the space and entering your body.

Start at east/Air, go clockwise, and use physical representations of the elements at the corresponding direction to make your circle.

Cast a circle by marking it out with salt, crushed up eggshells, sand, crystals, candles, or trace one with your finger.

A circle can also be cast using the elements.

HOW TO
Cast a Circle

A circle is something that is often cast before a spell or ritual—it helps stop any negative or unwanted energies coming from outside that could affect you and your workings. Casting a circle before a spell or ritual also helps to concentrate the energy you are raising into one small space, stop this energy from escaping, and intensify its effects.

Some Witches cast circles for every spell and ritual they perform, whereas others only cast a circle when the magick they are making requires extra protection, such as a banishing or cutting-the-cord spell. Other Witches don't use them at all. As your Craft and practice develops, you'll get a better feel for what is best for you, and it's important to do what feels right. Here are two of my favorite ways to cast a circle.

CASTING A SIMPLE CIRCLE
You can cast a circle by marking it out with salt. Although this is a traditional method, I don't recommend using salt outside. It will kill plants, insects, and small animals, so it is best to use crushed-up eggshells or sand. A circle can also be marked out using crystals, candles, visualization, and even a length of string or ribbon to make a circle around where you are going to work. A simple circle can be marked out with a wand or an athame (a ceremonial blade) and even just traced with your finger, which is good to know if you're ever in a fix and need to cast a circle quickly and easily.

CASTING A CIRCLE USING THE ELEMENTS
Start facing east and place a feather, incense, or other symbol of the element Air at this point on the floor around your workspace. Next, moving clockwise, turn south. Use a candle (or any other appropriate object) to represent Fire and place it on the floor at the south point. Next, face west and use a glass of water to represent Water—place this (or any other symbol for Water) on the floor at the west point. Finally, turn to face north and place a cup of soil or another representation of Earth at this point around your workspace to complete the circle.

When you have laid all four elements down to make your circle, while still facing north, visualize energetic white light from the Earth coming up through your feet, and entering your body. Let this light flow from your body and into the circle, filling it up. I often use these words at the end: "The elements of Air, Fire, Water, and Earth come together. I cast this circle of protection and power above, below, and within."

HOW TO CALL
the Elements

Calling the elements, otherwise known as "Calling the Quarters" and "Calling the Guardians of the Watchtowers," is a way of asking the four elements from the four different directions to lend their power to our spells or rituals. The Guardians of the Watchtowers are guardians of the elements. They are called upon in ceremonial and Neopagan magickal traditions and share the characteristics of the elements with which they are associated. They are not deities but are otherworldly figures that, if asked, can join you in your magickal workings and give them a boost of extra energy.

It is completely up to you as to which name you call upon to ask the elements to lend their power, if you choose to call upon them at all. If you want to call upon the elements but are not comfortable calling on the Guardians of the Watchtowers, you can simply call upon the elements themselves. It could be something as simple as saying, "Elements of Air/Fire//Water/ Earth, I call upon you," each time you place the representations of the elements down on the floor as you cast your circle. It doesn't really matter what words you use to call either the elements or the guardians, just be respectful

Many Witches call in the elements starting with north, as it represents Mother Earth, but other traditions call in the elements from the east, the direction of the sunrise. Go with what resonates with you the most.

Once your circle is cast, cleanse the area before you begin your spell or ritual. This can be done by burning herbs such as rosemary or juniper, or by using visualization or sound.

Element of Earth,

I call upon you

Element of Water,

I call upon you

START HERE

Element of Air,

I call upon you

HOW TO
CALL THE
ELEMENTS

Element of Fire,

I call upon you

HOW TO CLOSE A CIRCLE
& Dismiss the Elements

Closing a circle, also known as opening a circle, is carried out after your spell or ritual is finished. It's known as opening a circle because it's a way of releasing all the energy you have raised through your magickal workings into the universe. If you have cast your circle using only the elements, the circle is closed using the elements in the opposite order you called on them.

You could use these words for each element, "Thank you, Earth/Water/Fire/Air, for your presence in my circle and aiding my magick. You are free to go but most welcome to stay." Say these as you move anticlockwise around the circle, picking up the representations of the elements you have used in turn. As you do, visualize your circle opening up as you close it, element by element.

If you have called on the Guardians of the Watchtowers, start at north/Earth and work backwards around the circle, thanking and saying goodbye to the Guardians one by one in the same manner as you did to dismiss the elements themselves. You could use something like this, "Guardians of the Watchtowers of the north/west/south/east, spirits of the Earth/Air/Fire/Water, thank you for your presence in my circle and for aiding my rite. Goodbye and farewell."

You could mark out the circle in a physical way, begin at north/Earth and move anticlockwise around the circle, either by sweeping up any loose material such as salt, eggshells, or sand, or picking up items such as crystals and extinguishing candles. If you have used visualization to cast your circle, visualize the circle opening from north/Earth and moving anticlockwise around the circle until it is fully opened, and visualize that the white light has been absorbed into your surroundings and beyond. If you have used your finger or an athame to cast your circle, retrace the circle backwards and visualize the circle opening.

Once you have learned the basic principles of opening and closing a circle, as well as calling and dismissing the elements, you can shape them to suit your individual practice. You can modify the words of the examples I've used here to something that reflects your Craft and personality, just as long as the words are respectful.

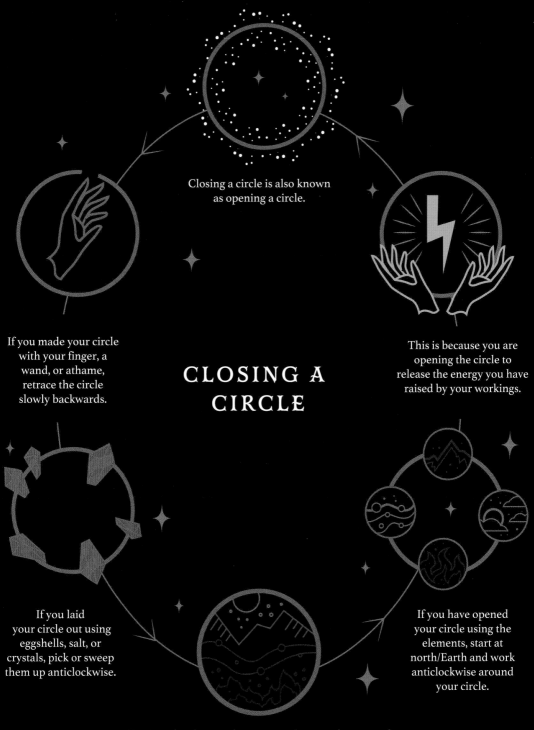

Closing a circle is also known as opening a circle.

This is because you are opening the circle to release the energy you have raised by your workings.

If you made your circle with your finger, a wand, or athame, retrace the circle slowly backwards.

CLOSING A CIRCLE

If you laid your circle out using eggshells, salt, or crystals, pick or sweep them up anticlockwise.

If you have opened your circle using the elements, start at north/Earth and work anticlockwise around your circle.

Remove the elemental representations one by one and say thank you to them for their assistance.

MAGICK IS A BALANCING ACT.
BALANCE IS A MAGICKAL ACT.

AFTER-SPELL
Care

After casting a spell and finishing your magickal workings, we can sometimes feel drained. It's also not unusual to feel physically unwell after completing a spell. Headaches, exhaustion, anxiety, and feeling energetically and physically "off" are common symptoms. This is not just relevant to those at the start of their Witchcraft journey, but it can happen to the more experienced witch, too. I've certainly had many instances over the years where I haven't felt great after a spell. But the good news is that there is something we can do about it!

Generally, the main reason why you might feel like this after a spell is because you undertook your spell work when your energy was not properly balanced. This is all part of knowing your own energy and knowing when your energy needs some recalibration. To avoid these kinds of feelings, it's important that you make sure you cleanse and ground yourself properly before and after a spell.

To cleanse myself, both before and after a spell or ritual, my go-to herbs are lavender, rosemary, and pine needles, but there are so many others to choose from. You can either burn them as loose incense on a charcoal disc, or, as I prefer, bind a bundle of these herbs together with string and light the end so it smolders. Burn enough so that you are surrounded by the smoke from head to toe—this will also cleanse the room of its energies. You can also cleanse with sound, for example, with the ringing of a high-pitched bell, or with light, by perhaps lighting a white candle and sitting in its glow until you feel lighter in body, mind, and spirit.

Grounding is important too, so you won't be unbalanced as you begin your spell, and afterward to make sure that if, for some reason your spell work has affected your energy, you can rebalance it before it can have a negative effect on you. You can use the grounding exercise found on page 170 before and after a spell.

You can also try this simple method that uses the five senses. Sit down somewhere comfortable and look around you and identify the following: 5 things you can see, 4 things you can feel, 3 things you can hear, 2 things you can smell, 1 thing you can taste. This method brings your mind into the present moment and helps you rebalance your energy. Take your time—don't rush. Sometimes, I also find a grounding ritual bath using salt, rosemary, lavender, and patchouli to be helpful after a spell that has wiped me out.

2

THE FOUR ELEMENTS

The four classic elements of Earth, Air, Fire, and Water play a central role in the practice and beliefs of Witchcraft. They are at the heart of all existence and, together, they are the earthly energies of nature that affect every single living thing on the planet. They are the forces of Mother Nature herself, and through our relationship with the elements, we can strengthen and deepen our connection to Mother Earth and the natural world.

Connecting to the elements individually or collectively can bring many benefits, both mundane and magickal. The elements can also help to ground and balance our own personal energies, improve our sense of well-being, and can be used as tools for self-care. We are all born under one of the four elements, based on our zodiac sign, but this doesn't necessarily mean that it's the element you will feel the most connected to. This chapter will help you to connect to the four individual elements through a selection of simple spells and rituals selected from my grimoire.

HOW TO CONSECRATE
USING THE ELEMENTS

START

1. Light the incense, which symbolizes Air, and the candle to symbolize Fire.

2. Take the tool you want to consecrate, and place it in a bowl of soil or salt or sprinkle it over it as you focus on the qualities of Earth—stability, practicality, and security.

5. Pass the tool through the flame of the candle and focus on the qualities of Fire—inspiration, creativity, and passion.

4. Pass the tool through the smoke of the incense that represents Air and focus on the qualities of Air—intellect, logic, and communication.

3. You can do this silently or you can call each element. For example, "Energies of Earth, I consecrate this (name of the tool) and charge it with your powers. I purify it and make it mine."

6. Finally, splash your tool with water while thinking about the qualities of Water—intuition, emotion, and perception.

7. End with these words if it feels right, 'By the powers of Earth, Air, Fire, and Water, I consecrate this (name of tool). I make it new, I make it mine.'

FINISH

HOW TO CONSECRATE
Using the Elements

The act of consecration is used to purify objects or tools such as an athame, boline (a white-handled ritual knife), or cauldron of any unwanted energies to get them ready for use during magickal workings. Essentially, consecration is a deep cleansing before you can align your energy to the energy of the tool. It also prepares the tool for work and interaction with the divine in whatever form this takes for you—gods, goddesses, the universe, or Mother Nature herself.

Consecration is used in several magickal traditions like Neopaganism, including Wicca, and some eclectic paths, but not all branches of Witchcraft require tools to be consecrated before use. Some practitioners believe that the act of directing their energy and intent into the tool as part of a spell or ritual is enough, so the decision whether to use consecration in your own Craft is down to you and if it feels right to do so.

My favorite way to consecrate my tools is to use the four elements because, each time, it helps to strengthen my connection with the power of the elements themselves and with the wider natural world. All you need are physical representations of the elements, such as soil or salt for Earth, incense for Air, a candle for Fire, and a glass of water for Water.

Caution: *Never leave a burning candle unattended and always burn candles out of the reach of children and pets. Always place candles in an upright position on a secure heat resistant surface and keep candles apart and away from draughts, flammable materials, sources of heat and overhanging objects.*

EARTH

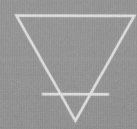

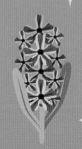

CRYSTALS
carnelian, diamond, emerald,
fluorite, green moss agate,
green aventurine, jade,
jasper (not red), malachite,
tiger's eye, tourmaline

EARTH THEMES
stability, practicality,
reliability, dependability,
grounding, strength, loyalty,
finances, wealth, material world,
certainty, health matters,
the body, senses

HERBS AND PLANTS
Bay leaves, basil, chamomile,
cypress, hawthorn, honeysuckle,
hyacinth, jasmine, mugwort,
oakmoss, patchouli, pine needles,
primrose, vervain

ZODIAC SIGNS
Taurus, Virgo,
Capricorn

TAROT SUIT
Pentacles

COLORS
green, brown

DIRECTION
north

SEASON
fall

TOOLS
salt, herbs,
crystals, soil

EARTH *Magick*

The Earth is the ground on which we stand and make our home. It is a source of life for every living thing on the planet. It supports, sustains, and stabilizes, and the soil is where the neverending cycle of the harvest occurs. It's no wonder that the element Earth is associated with stability, strength, security, productivity, abundance, and prosperity. The Earth is not just the ground beneath our feet, but is the trees, rocks, caves, fields, and crystals, as well as the plant and animal life around us.

Earth is connected to the zodiac signs Taurus, Virgo, and Capricorn because they are all practical, methodical, and value stability—all characteristics of the element itself. Earth is also associated with the suit of Pentacles in a tarot deck because it is the suit that represents the Earth-like themes of wealth, health, and the material world.

RITUALS TO CONNECT TO EARTH

Connecting to the element Earth has many mundane and magickal benefits. The first is the grounding effects that Earth can bring, which can have a profound impact on our mental, physical, and spiritual well-being. Walking barefoot or laying down on the earth is a simple and easy way of grounding yourself. Going for a walk and getting out into nature is another way.

Even walking around your local area, looking at gardens, window boxes, and flowerpots can have the same grounding impact.

Another way to connect to the element Earth is to grow something from seed or replant something more established in your garden. If you don't have a garden, you could grow something in a pot or in a window box. It's a chance to get your hands dirty and feel the soil between your fingers as you tend to and watch your seeds and plants grow.

Earth is easy to incorporate in physical form on an altar and is a great way to start to build up a relationship with this element. If you already have an altar, or if you want to make an altar specifically just for Earth, use items such as crystals, rocks, flowers, leaves, moss, or even a dish of soil or salt to connect to the element Earth, or display a tarot card from the Pentacles suit.

You can use your altar as a meditation aid. Spend 10 minutes a day interacting with the items, perhaps holding the crystals or putting your fingers into a bowl of soil. Blending your own incense to burn during your meditation, using herbs and flowers aligned with this element, is another great way of connecting with earthly energies. I love a blend of 2 parts pine needles, 1 part patchouli, 1 part honeysuckle flowers, 1 part cypress, and a pinch of salt.

EARTH SPELL-BAG
for Prosperity

The element of Earth can be used in several magickal ways. It's common practice for the remnants of spells and rituals to be buried at the end of some magickal workings. Returning them to the earth is a way in which to end a spell. If you bury spell remnants, make sure to bury only biodegradable ingredients such as incense ashes, paper, herbs, and flowers. I use a small plant pot with a lid, filled with soil where I don't grow anything but use it to bury non-biodegradable items such as candle wax, as well as spell remnants, such as salt, that would damage the environment. The Earth element is also cleansing. Burying an object in the ground for 24 hours will remove any negative or unwanted energies attached to it.

Earth spell-bag for prosperity

(A small drawstring bag or pouch
(1 or more of the following herbs: bay leaves, basil, chamomile, mint, thyme
(1 or more of the following crystals: citrine, green aventurine, jade, malachite
(Pen and paper
(Coins (in your country's currency)

Method

1. Focus on the kind of prosperity you want to attract. Think about how you'll feel once you have attained this abundance. Keep your intentions realistic and remember it is important that you do all you can on a practical level to bring about the prosperity you desire.

2. Cleanse the bag then take a generous pinch of each herb and place it into the bag.

3. Cleanse the crystals and then add them to the bag.

4. On the piece of paper, write about the specific kind of prosperity you want. Is it help to get a new job or a promotion? Do you need money to pay the bills or for something specific? When you've finished, fold the piece of paper up so it's small enough to fit into the bag.

5. Finally, add a few cleansed coins to the pouch.

6. Tie the drawstring so the contents are safe inside. As you do, you can repeat these words three times (or modify them to suit your needs): "prosperity flow, prosperity grow, money shine, money is mine."

7. Carry the bag with you, close to your wallet, until the spell is complete, and you have attracted the prosperity you wanted. Return the biodegradable ingredients to the earth by burying them in the ground. Cleanse the crystals, ready to be used again.

AIR

CRYSTALS
agate, amber, amethyst,
aquamarine, blue lace agate,
chrysocolla, citrine, clear quartz
turquoise, topaz, jasper,
pumice, fluorite

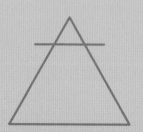

AIR THEMES
communication,
intellect, logic,
movement, reason,
thinking, knowledge,
objectivity

HERBS AND PLANTS
benzoin, clover, caraway,
cinnamon, dandelion, frankincense,
lemongrass, lemon balm,
lavender, mint, marjoram,
pine, parsley, sage

ZODIAC SIGNS
Gemini, Libra,
Aquarius

TAROT SUIT
Swords

COLORS
white, blue, yellow, purple

E

DIRECTION
east

SEASON
spring

OBJECTS
bells, chimes,
fragrance, smoke,
feathers

AIR *Magick*

Air can't be seen yet it's present at every moment of our existence. Without it, we could not exist at all. Air is the force of life for every living being on the planet, yet at the same time, it can also be incredibly destructive in the form of storms, gales, and hurricanes. In the Craft, it is represented by birds and feathers and magickal tools such as wands, incense, bells, and music.

Air is connected to the zodiac signs Gemini, Libra, and Aquarius because they share the characteristics of intellect and communication. Air is also associated with the suit of Swords in a tarot deck because it is the suit that represents the Air-like themes of intellect, and knowledge.

RITUALS TO CONNECT TO AIR

Using your breath is one of the easiest ways to connect to the element of Air. Sit somewhere quiet where you won't be disturbed and focus on your breathing—breathe in for 2 seconds and breathe out for 2 seconds, then breathe in for 3 seconds and breathe out for 3 seconds. Continue with this pattern until you reach 10, noticing the flow of cool air when you breathe in and warm breath out. You might find it beneficial to visualize the air coming in and flowing out as different colors. The great thing about this is it

can be done at any time and place and, if practiced regularly, it can help you to connect more deeply with the Air element.

Incorporating the Air element into your altar or creating one solely dedicated to this element is another simple way to connect. You can use crystals, objects, and herbs from the illustration opposite, as well as pictures of flying creatures such as dragonflies, faeries, and butterflies.

Burning an incense blend aligned to the energies of Air is a wonderful way to interact with this element and its free movement of energy, as we watch the smoke slowly rise and swirl. Incense smoke shows that Air isn't a fixed entity like Earth, but represents movement and flow, and just as the incense smoke dissipates quickly, those spells that call upon the powers of Air usually have short-term effects.

I love to make my own incense using equal parts of benzoin, lavender, lemon balm, and mint. Use the incense and the representations of Air on your altar as meditation aids and sit quietly for 10 minutes a day, thinking about the qualities of Air, watching the smoke, and feeling the flow of your breath. Ring chimes, bells, or play appropriate music if it helps you connect.

AIR SPELL-JAR
for Communication

You can use the wind to cleanse yourself of anything that doesn't align to your highest good. Stand in your garden or an open space like a park and, as you feel the wind, visualize it blowing any unwanted energies away. Raise your arms open wide if it feels right to do so. You can cleanse items such as crystals and tools in this way—simply leave them in your garden, secured safely but exposed to the wind for as long as necessary to cleanse. When an object feels energetically heavy, then it needs cleansing. After cleansing, the energy attached to it will feel lighter and brighter.

Wind can also be used to end a spell and return biodegradable spell ingredients back to the earth. Things such as incense ash or herbs can be returned to Mother Nature by throwing them to the wind. Just be sure to throw them so the wind blows it away from you!

Air spell-jar for communication
You will need:
- ☾ Clean jar (any size)
- ☾ 1 or more of the following dried herbs : cinnamon, dandelion, lemon balm, mint, rosemary
- ☾ 1 or more of the following crystals: blue lace agate, chrysocolla, clear quartz, turquoise
- ☾ Pen and paper
- ☾ 1 yellow candle

METHOD
1. Cast a circle and call the elements if it feels right to do so.
2. Use a clean, dry, cleansed jar and, when you add the ingredients, focus on your intentions of opening better lines of communication with those in your life. Visualize what it will be like when you can communicate your wants, needs, and ideas more clearly to others.
3. Add the herbs to the jar. Make sure all the herbs are fully dried before using them, so the contents don't mold.
4. Add the cleansed crystals and place them on top of the herbs.
5. If it feels right, write on a piece of paper in detail the ways in which you want to communicate better. When you've finished, fold up the paper and add it to the jar.
6. When you've finished creating your jar, close the lid. Burn a yellow candle and drip the wax all around the lid to fully seal it and finish the spell.
7. Keep the jar in a room where you spend most of your time with others to act as a reminder to strengthen the intentions you made. If small enough, keep the bottle with you throughout the day so it can work its magick.

FIRE

CRYSTALS
bloodstone, carnelian,
fire opal, garnet,
pyrite, red jasper,
ruby, rhodochrosite

FIRE THEMES
passion, movement, strenth,
action, power, willpower, courage,
sexuality, lust, destruction

PLANTS, HERBS AND SPICES
allspice, basil, calendula, cilantro,
cinnamon, cloves, cumin,
frankincense, ginger, juniper,
lemon, lime, nettle,
orange, poppies, saffron

ZODIAC SIGNS
Aries, Leo,
Sagittarius

TAROT SUIT
Wands

COLORS
red, yellow,
orange, gold

S
DIRECTION
south

SEASON
summer

TOOLS
athame, candles, sword,
wand, dagger, flames

FIRE Magick

The element of Fire, represented by the Sun and its warmth, makes our very existence on this planet possible. Without its heat, life on Earth would be impossible. Fire was life giving to our early ancestors and it is still important to our lives today: we use fire to cook with, to heat our homes during the colder seasons, and its light enables us to continue life after the Sun has set. Fire represents movement (think of the way the flame of a candle dances and flickers in a breeze) and transformation, as well as strength and creativity. It has the power to melt solids, quickly changing it from one form to another. In the Craft, it is symbolized by magickal tools such as a dagger, candles, as well as the suit of Wands in a tarot deck.

Fire is connected to the zodiac signs Aries, Leo, and Sagittarius because they are all passionate, creative, and energetic. Fire is also associated with the suit of Wands in a tarot deck because it is the suit that represents the Fire-like themes of strength and action.

RITUALS TO CONNECT WITH FIRE

There are many ways to connect to the element of Fire, but one of my favorite ways is to go for a nature walk on a sunny day and spend some time charging up my energies in the sunlight. Just as the moonlight can be used to charge magickal items such as crystals, the Sun's light can be used to energize our bodies and provide a boost of energy. Even sitting in the Sun for 10 minutes can really make a difference.

Setting up an altar dedicated to Fire is another great way to help you connect with the element. Like all altars, it's up to you as to what you want to include, but orange, red, yellow, or golden candles, an athame or knife, and flowers such as sunflowers are all traditional ways to physically represent Fire on your altar. Use this altar like the ones for Air and Earth—as a meditation aid to help you connect with Fire in a deeper and more profound way. Stare into the flames, watch them dance, and feel their warmth as you think about the qualities and powers of Fire. As you do, burn this incense blend of 2 parts frankincense, 1 part cinnamon, 1 part clove, and 1 part orange, lemon, lime peel to help to strengthen this connection.

You may find it easier to connect to the element Fire at some point during Imbolc, Lammas, Beltane, and Samhain, the four Fire festivals of the Pagan Wheel of the Year. During these times, bonfires are traditionally lit, and fire forms a central part in celebrations. As Fire is aligned to the summer season, you might find you connect easier to this element during the hotter months of the year.

FIRE CLEANSING
Candle Spell for Purification

In Witchcraft, Fire is known for its purifying effects. Passing an item or tool such as a boline through the flame of a candle will remove any physical and energetic impurities attached to it. Lighting a white candle is a simple way to purify a room. Burn one near the front door of your home when you have visitors as it will cleanse them as they enter. Fire can also be used to end a spell. Its destructive ability can be harnessed to burn spell ingredients, turning them into ash that can be returned to the earth.

Fire cleansing candle spell

You will need:

- ☾ Cloves and 1 or more of the following dried herbs: basil, cinnamon, rosemary, thyme
- ☾ 3 white candles
- ☾ A teaspoon of oil
- ☾ A small heatproof bowl
- ☾ Pen and paper

METHOD

1. Cast a circle and call the elements, if it is your tradition.
2. Grind up the herbs to a rough powder.
3. Rub some oil into the white candles from bottom to top, then roll them in the ground-up herbs so they stick.
4. Take a small handful of cloves and push some into all 3 candles.
5. Place the candles in a heatproof bowl, then sprinkle the remaining herbs around them in the bowl before lighting the candles.
6. On a piece of paper, write down in as much detail as you can about the things in your life that no longer serve you that you want to be cleansed from. Imagine the liberation and growth you'll experience once they are no longer holding you back.
7. When you've finished, burn the paper in the flames. As you do, visualize what you want to let go and how it will come to fruition. Drop the ashes of the paper around the candles with the ground-up herbs. Focus on the candle flames and your intentions for the spell as you watch the candles burn out.
8. Mix the ashes and herbs together and bury them in the ground somewhere in your yard. You should throw away the candle remnants as they're non-biodegradable, so are best not buried in the Earth.

WATER

CRYSTALS
amethyst, aquamarine, beryl,
bloodstone, blue tourmaline,
blue topaz, fluorite, laboradite,
lapis lazuli, moonstone, opal

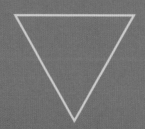

WATER THEMES
emotion, intuition, healing,
psychic abilities, love,
unconscious mind,
fertility, reflection, lunar energy,
deep feelings

HERBS AND PLANTS
catnip, comfrey, eucalyptus,
fern, gardenia, gernaium,
lily, lilac, lotus mugwort,
rose, seaweed,
water moss, willow

ZODIAC SIGNS
Pisces, Cancer,
Scorpio

TAROT SUIT
Cups

COLORS
blue, silver,
white, grey,
aquamarine

W

DIRECTION
west

SEASON
winter

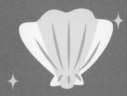

TOOLS
cauldron, chalice,
bowl, hag stones, shells

WATER
Magick

We live on a planet where 71% of its surface is water. It exists in solid, liquid, and gas form and sustains all life—without water, every living thing on Earth would die. Water symbolizes movement, emotions, healing, and intuition. It's a great element to work with during the winter months—when the temperatures drop and water freezes, you can use it as time to reflect. It also makes it a good time to do shadow work (see Chapter 8). Shadow work is a way to understand yourself better—by confronting those things in your life you may be ignoring, or hiding, and confronting those you are frightened of. While this is never easy, connecting with Water can help facilitate the process.

Water is connected to the zodiac signs Pisces, Cancer, and Scorpio because they are reflective and feel deeply. Water is also associated with the suit of Cups in a tarot deck because it is the suit that represents the Water-like themes of emotion and perception.

RITUALS TO CONNECT WITH WATER

Spending time near a natural source of water is one of the easiest ways to connect to this element. Whether that be ocean, river, or lake, being close to a natural source of water that's local to you, where you can visit regularly, will help you to build up a relationship. How you interact with water is based on what feels right for you—you could place your hand in the water, dip a toe, or even swim in it (if it's safe to do so). If you don't live near a natural source of water, bathing and showering at home as you consciously focus on the cleansing (or other) properties of water is a simple ritual that's easily incorporated into your day—the mundane can be changed into the magickal. Even entering a swimming pool allows you to connect with the flow and movement of water and can be transformed into a spiritual practice.

As with all the elements, incorporating water into your altar or sacred space is a great way to connect with Water. A simple bowl of water is enough, but you can add other items such as a cup, cauldron, seashells, driftwood, sea glass, sand, hag stones (a stone with a naturally occuring hole through it), coral, crystals like moonstone and aquamarine, and blue, white, and silver candles. They can be used as meditation aids; I find meditating with my hands submerged in a bowl of water very helpful when I want to connect with this element. Burn this incense blend to help strengthen your connection—2 parts myrrh, 1 part vanilla, 1 part rose petals, 1 part ylang-ylang, and 1 part thyme.

WATER RITUAL BATH
to Enhance Intuition

Water has so many uses in Witchcraft. Moonwater is great for cleansing and to add a boost of energy to your spells and rituals. You can drink with it, bathe in it, and water plants, too. To make moon water, leave a jar of clean drinking water (with a lid) in the light of a full Moon to charge for the night.

Depending on its origin, water has a variety of different properties and is associated with different kinds of magick:

RAIN WATER—protection, cleansing, change, growth

STORM WATER—emotional change, motivation

DEW—fertility, beauty, love, health, peace.

SUN WATER—strength, creativity, vitality, positivity

RIVER WATER—banishing, cleansing, change, energy

SEA WATER—healing, banishing, protection

SNOW—transformation, balance, purity, endings

ICE—transformation, creativity

LAKE/POND WATER—self-reflection, peace, spirituality

CAUTION: Do not drink or ingest any of these types of water unless specifically instructed to elsewhere in this book.

Water ritual bath to enhance intuition

You will need:

- ☽ 1 or more of the following plants or herbs: mugwort, rose petals, calendula
- ☽ Muslin bag (optional)
- ☽ Full moon water
- ☽ 1 purple candle
- ☽ 1 or more of the following crystals, cleansed: amethyst, bloodstone, labradorite, fluorite

CAUTION: If you have sensitive skin which is prone to allergic reactions, always perform a patch test with an infusion or decoction of the herb(s) you want to use in your ritual bath first.

METHOD

1. Take a tablespoon of each of the herbs or plants (dried or fresh)— and add to a full, warm bath.

2. Alternatively, place the herbs into a muslin or cotton drawstring bag and place that into the bath instead, if you don't like the idea of herbs floating around your bath water.

3. Next, add the moon water—use as much as you feel you need, from a little to a lot.

4. Light the purple candle (place it near the bath) and arrange the cleansed crystals in a circle around it.

5. Enjoy your bath, keeping your intentions focused on your intuition.

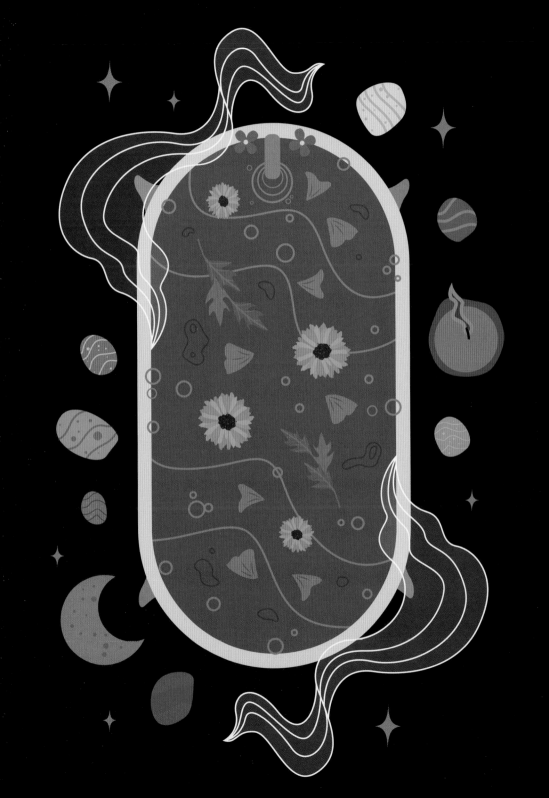

3

THE FOUR SEASONS

Everyone has a favorite season, a time of year where we feel more connected to the natural world than at any other. Mine is Fall. I feel that as nature is winding down and showing us her final glorious colors, I'm waking up from my slumbers.

Although this chapter isn't about the Wheel of the Year, it's important to place the seasons in the wider practice of Witchcraft. The Wheel of the Year, the yearly cycle of eight seasonal celebrations, known as Sabbats, is observed by many Pagans and Witches. There are four Sabbats based on the agricultural calendar. They are known as cross-quarter days or fire festivals (Imbolc, Lammas, Samhain, and Beltane), and there are four Sabbats based on the solstices and equinoxes known as quarter days (Yule, Ostara, Litha, and Mabon), which are midpoints between the fire festivals. They are aligned to the changing of the seasons and represent the points where the Sun is at the height of its power (Litha/Summer Solstice) and when the Sun is furthest away (Yule/Winter Solstice). Ostara (Spring Equinox) and Mabon (Fall Equinox) are midpoints where the night and day are at equal length.

The seasons play a big part in the practice of Witchcraft, and it's your choice as to which Sabbats you choose to celebrate.

FALL
Magick

Fall stretches between the Sabbats of Mabon and Yule, which fall between September and December in the Northern Hemisphere, and between March to June in the Southern Hemisphere.

Fall has many symbolic meanings within the practice of Witchcraft and is associated with certain kinds of magick. Aligning yourself and your Craft to the seasons can add power to your magick but can also help you connect with Mother Nature's cycle.

As nature prepares to sleep and leaves start to fall, it's a reminder that there is beauty in (some) endings. Banishing and cutting-the-cord rituals align well with the energies of this season. It's also a good time to identify those things in your life that limit your ability to reach your highest potential so you can shed the things that no longer serve your life. When it comes to cleansing, spring is probably the first month you

might think about, but the fall energies are also good for removing the old to make way for the new.

Fall is the season where the natural world prepares for the coming of the harder winter months ahead. For animals, this might mean storing up food or finding a safe place to hibernate, but for us, this time is good for home and personal protection magick. As humans, we might not hibernate, but we can still mirror the energies of nature at this time of year by protecting ourselves and the place we live, in preparation for the approaching winter.

Apple magick is also a great way to connect with energies of this season. Apples represent guidance and wisdom and can be used in prosperity and abundance spells. Carve sigils into the apple skin and then bury it in the ground.

ALIGN

WITH NATURE

Practice acorn magick.

Assemble a fall altar
incorporating foraged
fall bounties.

CONNECTING
WITH
FALL

Prioritize rest
and self-care.

Take a cleansing ritual bath, lighting red,
orange, yellow, or white candles
to represent the season.

Create an ancestor altar
to help you remember and
connect with them.

CONNECTING WITH THE
Energies of Fall

Taking nature's lead and slowing down is a good way to connect to fall's energies. Modern life is hectic and full of its own stresses and pressures, but actively making time for yourself and for activities that nourish your soul can align you with the natural energies of the season as well as deepen your connection with yourself.

It can be hard to carve out this time when our schedules are full, but that makes it even more important to stop for a while, slow down, and look after ourselves better. Self-care is important—but it isn't just about face masks and bubble baths—it can also be about setting boundaries, learning how to say "no," nourishing your body with healthy food, and speaking with your authentic voice. Fall is the perfect time to focus on the things that honor and validate the person you are on an emotional, mental, physical, and spiritual level.

Acorn magick is a great way to connect to the energies of fall. Acorns can bring protection and good luck when carried as an amulet and, if carried in your pockets, can help banish loneliness and illness. Acorns can also attract prosperity and wisdom if placed near a window in your home.

Creating a fall altar or incorporating fall items, such as leaves, conkers, and chestnuts into your existing altar is a great way to connect with this season and encourage you to strengthen your relationship with the cycles of nature. Collect leaves of different colors, shapes, and sizes and make a collage or mobile to use on your altar, or as a meditation aid as you focus and connect with the fall energies.

Fall is about endings, so it's a perfect time to let go of the old to make way for what is coming into your life. This could be cleaning out a closet or taking a cleansing ritual bath. I love using 2 parts Epsom salts, 1 part lavender, 1 part rosemary, and 1 part rose petals while burning patchouli incense.

As Samhain approaches, the veil between this world and the next thins, making it a great time for any kind of divination, spirit work, and for honoring your ancestors. Create an ancestor altar with family photos, personal belongings from those who have passed or leave an offering of their favorite food or drink. Honoring your ancestors doesn't have to be a ritual just for Samhain—it's something you can do at any time of the year, but the thinning of the veil throughout the fall months makes it easier to connect to the spirit world.

WINTER *Magick*

Winter stretches from Yule (or the Winter Solstice) to Ostara, the first day of spring, which lasts from December to April in the Northern Hemisphere and June to September in the Southern Hemisphere. It's the time where the days get shorter, and darkness overtakes light. After the colorful glory of fall, winter is a stark contrast—the trees are bare, it's cold, and the natural world is dormant and still. Fall energies urged us to slow down, but now winter is here, these energies want us to stop and rest. This season points us to look inward and focus our energy on ourselves, making it another good season for shadow work (see Chapter 8) and working on inner healing.

Rest can be a beautiful and magickal ritual, and it's something we don't often make enough time for. We might feel the instinctive urge to slow down and withdraw as the nights grow longer and our bodies try to tell us what they need. We are in tune with the natural world more than we know but the busyness of modern life can override this connection. Slowing down, resting, and being reflective is the ideal way to give yourself the space and time to just "be." If you feel the need to slow down, go with the flow and honor your feelings because the more you do this, the greater connection you will build with winter and its magick but also with the neverending rhythm of the seasons. Journaling is a great way to be reflective and get your thoughts down on paper.

Creating an altar to reflect the changing of the seasons is a physical way to connect to winter. Decorations such as pinecones, pine needles, colors of white, red, green, or silver, and candles are all great additions to any winter altar. Even lighting just one candle and using the time to reflect and be still for a while can help to sync your natural cycles with that of Mother Earth, remembering you are a human *being* not a human *doing*.

Rest
IS
Beautiful

Practice shadow work.

Focus on
inner healing.

Use snowball magick to remove
unwanted energy.

CONNECTING
WITH
WINTER

Neutralize unwanted energy
with snow magick.

Melt ice to let go;
freeze it to bind.

Use pinecones to focus
your intentions.

CONNECTING WITH THE
Energies of Winter

If you live in an area of the world where it is cold enough in the winter for snow and ice, you can collect snow water to use for purification, cleansing, and healing. The way the snow falls can be used for different kinds of magick. If the snow falls softly, the snow can be used in magick related to peace and calm. If the snow falls in a heavy blizzard, this snow can be used to add power and energy to your magick.

Snow made into snowballs can be used to cleanse yourself of any unwanted or negative energy attached to you. As you form a snowball, visualize it pulling out any energy that shouldn't be around you. I visualize this energy being darker in color, which is neutralized when it is dragged into the white snowball.

You'll know you are cleansed when you start to feel lighter physically and mentally. When you are ready, throw the snowball as far away from you as possible. As you do, visualize the darker energy shooting away from you, leaving you deeply cleansed.

Ice is a powerful tool and has many uses. Melting ice is associated with letting go or shedding the things that don't serve us. Shattering ice can be used in banishing and cutting –the-cord spells. Freezing water, either kept outside if it's cold enough, or in the freezer, can be used in binding magick.

In the middle of winter in the Northern Hemisphere, we see the end of one calendar year and the start of a new. To honor this transition and look forward to the beginning of a new year, all you need is a pinecone and some very small strips of paper.

On the paper, write the intentions you have for the New Year and what you intend to achieve. Roll up the pieces of paper and push them in between the open scales of the pinecone. Use as many pieces of paper as you need or as many as your pinecone will allow. When it's filled, burn it on a fire. As the flames make the pinecone glow, focus on the intentions you have written on the pieces of paper. When it has cooled and turned into ash, bury it in the ground.

Winter, when the natural world hibernates, is a time to go inwards. We need to recognize our shadows as well as our light. Setting time aside for shadow work (see Chapter 8) where we can confront our darkness is a way to connect with the Winter energies, as well as understand yourself better.

SPRING
Magick

After the cold, dark months of the winter, we welcome the coming of spring. This season officially begins at Ostara, which falls at the end of March in the Northern Hemisphere and the end of September in the Southern Hemisphere. Mother Nature is waking up from her slumbers, the days are finally getting longer, and there are signs of life sprouting up everywhere. It's a time to celebrate the return of the Sun and, with it, the energy and vitality of the natural world. Now spring is here, nature is showing us how to shed the things that have died over the winter to make way for new growth.

Spring is ideal for magick relating to new beginnings, transformation, and setting intentions. Seed magick is a great way to work with the earth and feel the energy and vitality of the soil as the natural world wakes up. Plant seeds or spring bulbs with intention. As you care for and watch them grow, they represent your intentions as they slowly manifest. But you must also do the mundane work to make your intentions possible! You won't win the lottery without buying a ticket. It's the same with magick. The work you do is just as important as the magick itself—one supports the other.

Spring is also the perfect time to do prosperity work for the rest of the year. Prosperity is not just about wealth—it can also be good health, success, and personal growth. For a simple, earth-based prosperity spell you need a large green (or white) candle, an envelope, a piece of paper, some earth, mint, cinnamon, and basil. Take the envelope and place the coin and a small amount of earth inside. Grind up the herbs and sprinkle them onto the soil, mixing them well together.

As you do, think of the kind of prosperity you want to attract. You can even draw a prosperity sigil on the front. When you're ready, bury it in the ground somewhere in your yard or on your property. Rub a little oil on the green candle and roll it in the remaining ground-up herbs so they stick. Light the candle and focus on your intentions as it burns. Let it burn for 15 minutes and then extinguish it. Burn it for a short time every day to invite continued prosperity into your life until the candle has burned away. It's up to you how big your candle is, based on how many days you want it the spell to last.

Take a cleansing
ritual bath or shower.

Flush out stagnant energies
from winter by having
a spring clean.

CONNECTING
WITH
SPRING

Plant seeds or bulbs during
the Waxing Moon to
encourage growth.

Start a new project.

Create a spring altar.

CONNECTING WITH THE
Energies of Spring

As with the other seasons, creating an altar to honor spring is a great way to connect with the energies of this time of year. Potted bulbs, seeds, spring flowers, and ribbons are all wonderful additions to any spring altar, as are green, red, or pastel-colored candles. Your altar doesn't have to be complicated or take up lots of space; I prefer to add some simple spring flowers to the altar I use daily to keep me connected to the springtime energies.

Spring is the time where the days are getting longer. At the Spring Equinox, the days and the nights become perfectly balanced and are of equal length. I like to keep a black and a white candle on my altar to represent the balance between light and dark. I also do this during fall when there's balance between dark and light as we move into the dark half of the year.

Dandelions have so many magickal uses and, during the spring, you might see the bright yellow flower popping up in your garden, on fields and in hedges. They can be used for many kinds of magick, including those to boost creativity, inspiration, and courage.

I love to use dandelion roots in a roasted tea to boost divinatory insight. To make the tea from the roots, pull up the dandelions, cut off the stalk, rinse the roots thoroughly and place on a baking tray in the oven for 2 hours at 250°F (120°C). Let the roots cool, then use a coffee grinder or mortar and pestle to grind them down into a powder. When you're ready to drink it, place a tablespoon of the dandelion powder into a tea diffuser ball and steep in hot water until it reaches your preferred strength. Drink it before and during divination to give clarity of sight.

Spring is associated with cleaning—the process of removing the old to make way for the new. Whether this is physically cleaning your home or cleansing yourself of unwanted energies, it can help you connect to the very essence of spring and the promise of new beginnings. To create a protective house cleaner, mix one cup (250ml) of distilled white vinegar with half a cup of water (125ml), 5 drops of lemon essential oil, 5 drops of rosemary essential oil, and 5 drops of lavender oil. Make sure the surface won't be damaged by these ingredients before using, as some surfaces may be damaged by essential oils.

SUMMER
Magick

Summer falls between the Summer Solstice and the Fall Equinox, which is from June to September in the Northern Hemisphere and December to March in the Southern Hemisphere. The Sun is at the height of its power, and for many places in the world this means higher temperatures and brighter days. The good weather means we can get outside more. Nature is flourishing; the Earth's luscious green growth is abundant, and flowers are blooming everywhere. It's a time for magick associated with power and energy.

The Sun is a wonderful magickal tool that can be used in so many ways. You can make Sun water by placing a jar or bottle of clean drinking water in the sunlight to charge for a full day and bring it in before dark. It can be used for cleansing your space, tools, or altar and giving spells some extra power. It's also a great addition to healing magick, protection spells, and can be drunk when you need a boost of creativity.

The sunlight itself can be used to charge crystals and divination tools such as tarot cards and runes, although be careful because some crystals will fade and be damaged if put in direct sunlight (see page 105). After washing your clothes, put them out to dry in direct sunlight to absorb the protective energy of the Sun.

Sometimes we need a little help to get the creative energies flowing and summer is the ideal time for magick of this kind. The warmer months are fantastic for spells that either promote a specific type of creativity that is related to a project you're working on or for if you just want to welcome a greater sense of inspiration into your life and Craft.

To make a simple creativity spell jar, fill a jar in the size of your choice with nutmeg, rosemary, basil, and the crystals red jasper and citrine. Drip the wax of a yellow candle around the lid to seal the jar. I also like to include a symbol of the specific kind of creativity I need help with, for example, you could include a piece of paper with a musical note written on it to boost musical creativity. As you fill the jar, visualize what kind of inspiration you want to bring about and picture yourself and how you will feel when your creative juices are flowing. Keep it near, or if the jar is small enough, keep it in your pocket and give it a shake when you need some inspiration.

BLOOM AT
YOUR OWN PACE

Carry Fire crystals such as ruby,
red jasper, and fire agate
for energy.

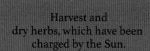

Harvest and
dry herbs, which have been
charged by the Sun.

CONNECTING
WITH
SUMMER

Set up a
summer altar.

Work with fire.

Align your magick with the
Sun phases and time of day.

CONNECTING WITH THE
Energies of Summer

Summer is aligned with the Fire element and the Summer Solstice is a Fire festival. To connect with the Fire element, you can light a bonfire and follow the traditional practice of jumping over it to benefit from its cleansing and purifying qualities. Or simply light a candle in a color associated with Fire, such as red, yellow, and orange, and meditate on the solar qualities of passion, courage, and strength.

Carrying crystals associated with the Fire element and the Sun, such as sunstone, red jasper, and carnelian, which have been left to charge in the sunlight, is a great way to connect with summer energies. They can be easily and discreetly carried with you and can help give boosts of energy. Recharge them regularly to keep them topped up with solar energy.

Setting up a summer altar helps connect to summer energies. Add candles in the colors associated with Fire, and flowers that are associated with the Sun such as sunflowers, marigolds, carnations, and lilies. Solar symbols are a great addition to any summer altar, as is fruit such as pineapples, tangerines, and pomegranates, as well as herbs such as rosemary, chamomile, cedar, meadowsweet, rue, and juniper. Even a vase of bright flowers is enough to celebrate the vibrant energies of summer.

The Summer Solstice is the best time to harvest and dry herbs. It's believed that they reach the height of their magickal and medicinal power at the same point the Sun reaches the peak of its energy, so get foraging and dry out what you find. Bunches of herbs are also given as gifts at the Summer Solstice.

Just like the Moon, the Sun has its own phases—sunrise, morning, noon, afternoon, and sunset. Align yourself to the different times of day and to how the strength and energy of the Sun feels and changes over this time.

Morning Sun corresponds to themes of expansion and growth, so to connect to the Sun at this point in the day could involve reading something new as a way to expand your knowledge. Midday Sun is at the peak of its strength—spells or rituals relating to power can connect you to its energies, or you could give your Sun safe crystals (see page 105) a sunbath to charge. Around the time of sunset, the Sun is decreasing in strength. Perform magick associated with reduction, endings, and truth at this time of day to help you connect with this phase.

TUNING INTO YOUR OWN
Seasons & Energy

It is important to understand that, as individuals, we all experience our own seasons and ebbs and flows of energy, and this doesn't always correspond with the four seasons of the natural world, the cycles of the Moon, or the Sabbats. Knowing your own energy and recognizing that we all experience unique seasons in life at different times is an essential skill that will help you to connect with yourself on a deeper level, and help you identify what your mind, body, and spirit needs, and how to provide it.

As Witches, there are many different natural cycles that help to shape our Craft, but there are many times where our own energy is different to these cycles. For example, the New Moon or spring is meant to be a time when our energy is renewed, but it's possible you could feel the very opposite of that sometimes. It doesn't mean that you don't have a good connection to the Moon or nature, or that you are any less of a Witch for feeling this way—all it shows is that we have our own energetic cycles. It gives you an opportunity to connect with your own energy on a deeper level and to honor it by giving yourself what you need at that time.

Honoring our own cycles is a crucial part of being a Witch. Sometimes you just need a little push to practice, and find yourself more energized for it, but other days, you risk pushing yourself too far if you ignore your energy levels. If you've planned a spell for days but when the day arrives and you feel drained or energetically unbalanced, it's a better idea to postpone your spell and wait for a time when your energy levels have been replenished and you're feeling more balanced. Physical illness, stress, anxiety, and depression are just some of the things that can knock your energy off balance. Casting a spell when your energy is all over the place or is low is likely not to work. Unbalanced energy is also likely to lead to unpredictable results.

Instead of casting a spell, your mind, body, and spirit need care and attention. It can take time to align yourself to your own cycles, particularly at the start of your Witchcraft journey, so be patient with yourself—it's certainly not a sign that you are less of a Witch or that this is the wrong path for you. Don't fight against it but instead learn to be guided by it and it will transform your Craft.

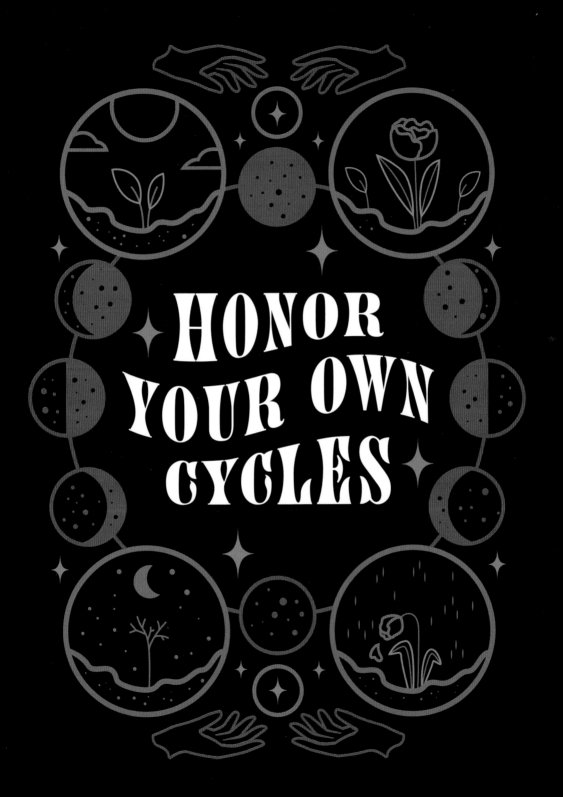

4

MOTHER EARTH'S MAGICK

The fruits of the natural world make powerful magickal ingredients. From herbs to resins, flowers, metals, and salt, they all have their specific magickal qualities and uses. Working with them can help to connect us and our Craft to the energies of Mother Nature herself.

Earth magick is a very traditional form of Witchcraft, which our ancestors used before us. They made the best of what they had to hand. They didn't have the luxury of being able to buy their herbs from the internet!

Natural magick is about connecting with the Earth and her energies on a deep level through the practice of your Craft. It's not just about a connection with the element of Earth or even the four elements combined. It includes all earthly energies that move around us as well as the physical gifts from Mother Nature, which include all the magickal ingredients you're about to read about!

In this chapter, you will learn about the magickal properties of a selection of earthly materials. It will also show you how to blend your own loose incense with a balanced fragrance based on the different notes of the herbs and flowers you use.

When working with plants, there are some ground rules you must follow. The recipes in this chapter are almost all for external use only. Do not consume any of the ingredients unless the recipe clearly states you can, and only then if you are sure that you will not have any allergic or other adverse reactions. If in doubt, seek medical advice. Never ingest or touch an unidentified herb. Always research your herbs before ingesting or making skin contact with them, and seek advice medical advice before before working with any plants if you are pregnant, suffer from any allergies, or have any health concerns. If you feel unwell or have any reactions to a plant, seek medical advice immediately. Be aware that some plants may also be dangerous to animals.

HERB AND SPICE GRIMOIRE

1. Allspice—Healing, money, energy, success, good luck
2. Cayenne Pepper—Banishing, cleansing, purification, removing obstacles, reversing hexes
3. Cedar—Healing, purification, psychic abilities, protection, money
4. Cilantro—Love, lust, healing, protection

HERB & SPICE
Grimoire

ALLSPICE *(Pimenta dioica)*

Allspice derives from a tropical member of the myrtle family and produces small white flowers and berries; both can be used in healing spells. The berries can be burned as incense for healing and are good to use in spells relating to wealth and finances. Add some allspice to a money spell jar or in a sachet and keep it in your wallet to attract good fortune. Allspice is a great ingredient in spells that attract good luck and business success. Sprinkle some in the four corners of the room where you work, whether home, office, or business. Allspice can also be added to any spell to bring a boost of energy and determination.

CAYENNE PEPPER *(Capsicum annuum)*

Cayenne pepper comes from the dried pods of chili peppers. It's used in banishing spells and for those who seek to reverse any kind of negativity. It can also be used in hexes, and curses, which makes it essential for reversing this kind of magick. Sprinkle cayenne around your home to break a curse, or boil it in water, let it cool, then use it to spiritually cleanse and purify inside your home. Add cayenne to spells that seek to remove obstacles that are preventing you attaining your goals. Adding it to any kind of spell will also help

to strengthen the effect of the herbs you use. ***CAUTION***: *keep cayenne away from eyes and delicate places to avoid irritation. Always wash your hands after handling.*

CEDAR *(Cedrus libani)*

Cedar is used in healing and purification. Burn it in a small bundle or use the twigs to make incense to release its purifying smoke. Burning it also helps to boost psychic abilities and attract wealth. Place some cedar in a pouch near your wallet to attract wealth. Cedar is protective—hang some above your front door to keep negative energies away. It can also be used as a talisman to represent long life and growth.

CILANTRO *(Coriandrum sativum)*

Cilantro, or coriander, is used in spells associated with love—use in red sachets carried on your person or in jars. Grind the seeds into a powder and add it to food or drink to attract and enhance feelings of love, lust, and sexual energy. Drinking it as a tea can also help to ease heartache after a breakup. Cilantro is associated with healing magick and can be worn to prevent headaches and migraines. It's used in protective magick. Grow it in your garden or inside in a pot to protect and bring peace to your home.

JUNPIER (*Juniperus communes*)

Juniper is highly protective and guards against theft. Hang some above your door to protect your home. Juniper can also be used for cleansing and to eliminate negative spirits. Grind it in a mortar and pestle and add to incense to release its cleansing smoke and invoke positive energy. Anoint yourself with juniper oil to remove any unwanted or negative energies. Add juniper to love spells and use the berries in pouches, charms, and oils to attract love, and to raise spiritual vibrations.

MARJORAM (*Origanum majorana*)

Use marjoram in love workings. Place it under your pillow to dream of your future love. It can also drive away illness and promote good health when carried in a pouch in your pocket or used in a ritual bath. Carry marjoram for protection or put it under your pillow to bring revealing dreams. Use in money spells to attract wealth. It's an herb of joy and can help lift our mood and alleviate sadness when used to infuse your bathwater every day for a week or when consumed in food. When eaten it can also strengthen feelings of love.

PARSLEY (*Petroselinum crispum*)

Parsley seeds, roots, and leaves can be used for purification and to communicate with spirits and the realms beyond this life if burned as incense or used in a ritual bath infusion. With its protective qualities, use parsley seeds on your altar to keep negative energies away or in a spell bag for personal protection. By wearing it as a charm and eating it in food, parsley helps to promote strength and vitality, increase fertility, invoke lust and passion, and attract good luck.

PATCHOULI (*Pogostemon cablin*)

Burning patchouli as incense has a grounding effect, brings a sense of emotional balance, and can connect you with the Earth and her energies. It also balances the root chakra. It's associated with money magick—use it to dress a green candle and burn it to attract wealth, or sprinkle it on the credit cards in your wallet to draw abundance and prosperity. Add patchouli to water and wash the floors in your house to bring calming and peaceful energies to your home.

HERB AND SPICE GRIMOIRE

2. 3.

1. 4.

1. Juniper—Protection, cleansing, love, raising vibrations
2. Marjoram—Love, good health, protection, dreams
3. Parsley—Purification, spirit communication, protection, fertility, good luck
4. Patchouli—Grounding, money, abundance, peace

PEPPERMINT (*Mentha piperita*)

Peppermint clears negative energy when burned as incense. Keeping peppermint on your altar will encourage good spirits to aid your workings. It's also associated with increasing psychic ability. Keep a few leaves with your tarot or oracle cards to keep them cleansed and to aid divination. Peppermint can help aid restful sleep and give glimpses of the future when placed in a dream pillow. Drinking peppermint tea before bed can also help this. Rub a peppermint leaf on your temples (be careful not to rub your eyes) to clear your mind and promote clarity.

RUE (*Ruta graveolens*)

Rue is a herb used to break hexes and curses and to ward off evil. Plant some near your front door to break any negative spells that may have been cast on the home or on those who live within. Rue helps to increase psychic abilities—burn dried rue as an incense, use in ritual baths, or place it over your third eye (the center of your forehead) to strengthen and develop second sight. Associated with healing, rue is added to good health and healing poppets, and sachets. **CAUTION**: *Fresh rue can irritate the skin, so always use it dried. If collecting your own rue from the wild or from your own living plant, handle it with care until it is fully dry, and always wash your hands after handling fresh rue.*

TARRAGON (*Artemisia dracunculus*)

Tarragon is a protective herb. Sprinkle it on the windowsills and doorways of your home for protection from thieves. It is also used to help increase confidence and is associated with magick connected to compassion and courage. Use it in a spell bag and carry it around in your pocket during the day. Tarragon is also used for banishing negative energies. Burn it as incense or eat in food to benefit from its cleansing abilities.

VALERIAN (*Valeriana officinalis*)

Valerian is well-known for its ability to bring calm, reduce anxiety, and aid sleep. Place some under your pillow for a restful night or drink as a tea before bed. It is best used in powdered form because of its strong smell—grind up the root and use in protection spells or pouches. It can also protect against the negative magick of others. Burned as incense, valerian can purify your altar or ritual space and help create a calm environment.

HERB AND SPICE GRIMOIRE

1. Peppermint—Psychic abilities, cleansing, sleep, clarity
2. Rue—Breaking hexes, psychic abilities, healing, good health
3. Tarragon—Protection, confidence, courage, banishing
4. Valerian—Calming, aiding sleep, protection, purification

FLOWER GRIMOIRE

2. 3.

1. 4.

1. Calendula—Protection, legal matters, dreams
2. Carnation—Breaking hexes, healing, love
3. Daisy—Love, divination, breaking spells
4. Elderflower—Healing, good health, protection, purification

FLOWER *Grimoire*

CALENDULA *(Calendula officinalis)*

Used for protection magick, calendula petals (also known as English marigolds), can be burned as incense and used in spell bags and jars. Plant them near your front door for protection from thieves. Calendula flowers can be added to a bath to help win the respect of everyone you meet. Associated with justice and legal matters, carrying the flowers into a court case can help to achieve a favorable outcome. To encourage prophetic dreams, sleep on a pillow filled with the flowers or add them to a tea blend you drink before bed.

CARNATION *(Dianthus caryophyllus)*

Carnations are protective and can break hexes. Burn them as incense to remove negative energy from a space. Use red and white flowers in your bath to bring stability to your love life. Carnations are associated with healing. Place a bunch in your bedroom to help you heal when you're ill. Use red carnations on your altar when performing healing spells or rituals. Carnations are best picked at noon when the Sun is at the height of its power.

DAISY *Bellis perenis (European), Chrysanthemum leucanthemum (American)*

The daisy is associated with love. Sleeping with daisies under your pillow is said to reignite an old love affair. Carrying or wearing a daisy attracts love. This love isn't the passionate kind—making daisies more suited to love spells for long-term relationships or love and platonic friendships. Daisies can also be used for simple divination. Ask a "yes or no" question then pull the petals off the daisy, one by one, alternating between yes and no, until you get to the last petal, which gives you your answer.

ELDERFLOWER *(Sambucus nigra)*

Elderflower has incredible healing properties. Add them to your bath or make an infusion to bring emotional and spiritual healing, and to help with mental and emotional stress. Add to a spell bag with dried rue and dill to promote good health and ward off illness. The flowers are also used in protection and purification incenses, and uncrossing spells. They can be used to break magick that has been cast against you.

GERANIUM *(Geranium maculatum)*

Geraniums are associated with love magick. Grind down pink geranium flowers and use them to dress a pink candle to open up the heart to love. It also helps to brings balance to passive and aggressive energies and helps grow acceptance. Use in a tea to neutralize any love spells placed on you. White flowers can be used in tea, ritual baths, and spell bags to increase fertility. Use red geranium flowers in protection sachets.

HIBISCUS *(Hibiscus)*

Hibiscus can be used in love magick. The flowers can be used in potpourri and spell pouches. Use red hibiscus flowers in incenses, sprays, spell bags, or brew in a tea to increase lust and passion. Yellow flowered hibiscus can be used to bring peace—use in a floor wash to bring harmony to your home. Purple flowered hibiscus are associated with psychic abilities and can enhance divinatory sight. Burn the petals as incense during divination.

HONEYSUCKLE *(Lonicera caprifolium)*

Burning honeysuckle as incense will attract wealth. Put the flowers in pouches around your home to attract prosperity. It's said that crushed honeysuckle flowers rubbed on the third eye (the middle of your forehead) will heighten psychic abilities. Even smelling the heady fragrance of the flowers can bring clarity, increase psychic powers, and strengthen intuition. Burn as incense when practicing divination to sharpen your second sight. With their protective qualities, growing them in your garden will bring good luck and protection.

JASMINE *(Jasminum grandiflorum)*

Burn as incense in the bedroom or place some under your pillow to induce prophetic dreams. Dress a candle with jasmine oil to bring psychic protection. Associated with money magick, put in a pouch with a coin and keep it near your wallet, or use jasmine oil to dress a green candle and burn it to attract wealth. Jasmine has a strong connection with love magick. Place the petals in a spell jar with honey to attract all forms of love into your life.

FLOWER GRIMOIRE

1. Geranium—Love, fertility, protection, balance
2. Hibiscus—Love, lust and passion, psychic abilities
3. Honeysuckle—Money, prosperity, psychic abilities, good luck
4. Jasmine—Prophetic dreams, money, love

MALLOW *(Malva sylvestris)*

Dried blue mallow flowers can be used in love spells and can be blended into incense or carried in a pouch to attract love and enhance sex magick. Mallow flowers are associated with protection and can be used in incenses. Steep mallow flowers in boiling water to make an infusion. Once cooled and drained, add the water to a spray for personal protection or use it to wash the windows in your house for home protection. Steep mallow in oil for two weeks to create a protection oil.

POPPY *(Papaver)*

Poppies have many uses and can be used in love, fertility, and money spells. They can also help with insomnia. Fill a pouch of poppy seeds and flowers and sleep with it under your pillow for a restful night's sleep. It is said that if you want to know an answer to a question, write it on a piece of paper and put it in a pouch with poppy seeds and the answer will appear somewhere in your dreams.

SUNFLOWERS *(Helianthus annuus)*

This bright and cheerful flower is a symbol of good luck. Take a ritual bath with sunflower petals or eat sunflower seeds to increase fertility. Sunflowers are associated with honesty—sleeping with a sunflower under your pillow can help you find the truth about a matter when you wake in the morning. The petals and seeds can be used for protection magick and carrying them in a pouch can help to protect against illness and promote good health.

FLOWER GRIMOIRE

1. Mallow—Love, protection
2. Poppy—Love, fertility, money, sleep
3. Sunflower—Good luck, truth, good health, protection

HERBS, FLOWERS, & SPICES
by Intention

This section is designed to make it easy to find the plants you need for spell work. If you are planning a spell but don't know what plants to use, look down the list of intentions below. Find the intention that aligns with your magick to identify the list of herbs, spices, and flowers you could use.

I have included a range of common plants so you can make the most of the things you have around you. I have also included plants connected to each of the four elements to make this a comprehensive collection of plants by intention. These commonly known correspondence are taken from Scott Cuningham's *Encyclopaedia of Magical Herbs* and I have also included herbs, spices and flowers I have found that work for each intention, based on my own practice.

Abundance
Bluebell, chamomile, ginger, honeysuckle.

Banishing
Angelica, basil, cayenne, cinnamon, comfrey, dried rue, frankincense, lilac, meadowsweet, mugwort, patchouli, peppermint, rose, rosemary, vervain, violet, yarrow.

Breaking love spells
Lily, lotus.

Breaking negative spells
Basil, chili pepper, hydrangea, thistle, wintergreen.

Clarity
Basil, clove, dandelion, dried rue, frankincense, honeysuckle, iris, jasmine, lavender, lemon balm, mullein, peppermint, rosemary, sage, sandalwood, sunflower.

Cleansing
Bay, cedar, cinnamon, eucalyptus, juniper, lavender, mugwort, rosemary.

Creativity
Cardamon, chamomile, cinnamon, daisy, lavender, lily, patchouli, peppermint, rose, rosemary, valerian, vervain.

Divination

Calendula, camphor, daisy, dandelion, dried rue, hibiscus, ivy, lavender, meadowsweet, mugwort, orris root, peppermint, rose, sage, thyme, vervain, wormwood, yarrow.

Fertility

Daffodil, dock, fern, geranium, grape, hawthorn, mustard, myrtle, patchouli, pine, pomegranate, poppy, sunflower.

Friendship

Clove, clover, gardinia, geranium, jasmine, lavender, passion flower, primrose, rosemary, sweet pea, yarrow.

Grounding

Chamomile, dandelion, lavender, rosemary, sage, sandalwood, vervain.

Happiness

Bergamot, calendula, catnip, cilantro, clove, frankincense, geranium, honeysuckle, hyacinth, jasmine, lemon balm, marjoram, mugwort, rose, sunflower, thyme, violet, yarrow.

Healing

Aloe, basil, daisy, dandelion, dried rue, fennel, frankincense, ginger, ginseng, ivy, jasmine, lavender, myrrh, nettle, peppermint, rosemary, sage, valerian.

Health

Camphor, caraway, cilantro, dried rue, fern, geranium, juniper, marjoram, nutmeg, thyme.

Intuition

Eyebright, fennel seeds, hibiscus, lavender, rosemary, skullcap, thyme.

Luck

Fern, four-leaf clover, heather, lavender, lilac, moss, nettle, patchouli, peppermint, poppy, star anise, sunflower, thyme, yarrow.

Money

Dandelion, dill, dock, fennel, honeysuckle, jasmine, lemon balm, marjoram, mint, nutmeg, patchouli, pine, poppy, sunflower, thyme, valerian, vervain.

Overcoming obstacles

Bluebell, cayenne, chicory root, hibiscus, myrrh, orris root, sage, witch grass, wormwood.

Prosperity

Basil, benzoin, cinnamon, ginger, patchouli, tulip.

Legal matters & justice

Buckthorn, calendula, hickory.

Love

Dried rue, hibiscus, hyacinth, jasmine, lavender, lemon balm, mallow, marjoram, poppy, rose, rosemary, skullcap, spearmint, thyme, tulip, valerian, vervain.

Protection

Agrimony, bay, caraway, carnation, cumin, eucalyptus, fern, heather, hyacinth, juniper, lavender, lilac, mugwort, myrrh, nettle, pepper, primrose, sage, thistle, wintergreen.

Psychic abilities

Catnip, cinnamon, clove, dandelion, frankincense, hibiscus, iris, jasmine, lavender, mugwort, mullein, myrrh, nutmeg, peppermint, rose, sandalwood, wormwood, yarrow.

Purification

Fennel, iris, lavender, peppermint, rosemary, thyme, turmeric, valerian, vervain.

Sleep

Cinquefoil, lavender, nutmeg, passion flower, peppermint, rosemary, valerian, vervain.

Strength

Carnation, cinnamon, comfrey, honeysuckle, lavender, mugwort, rosemary, rose, saffron, sunflower, sweet pea, thistle, thyme.

CELTIC TREE
Zodiac

The Celtic tree zodiac is based upon the belief system of the Druids. These Celtic priests had a profound connection to nature, and believed trees were a source of ancient and sacred wisdom. The Druids believed that the time and date of a person's birth was directly linked to their character and the formulation of their personality. The Celtic tree zodiac is based upon an ancient Moon calendar with 13 lunar cycles that link to 13 different Celtic trees, rather than the 12 signs of the Western zodiac system.

Each tree represents the characteristics of those born during this time, listed below.. Wood can also be incorporated into your Craft in a variety of ways. It can be added to incense and burned, and it can also be used to make tools such as wands, besoms, boline handles, and carved statues.

Rowan
Idealistic, spiritual, leader not a follower, artistic.

Ash
Free thinkers, realistic, logical, compassionate.

Alder
Independent, competitive, outgoing, confident.

Willow
Guarded, articulate, natural teachers, intuitive.

Hawthorn
Creative, good sense of humor, passionate.

Oak
Optimistic, determined, good leaders, motivated.

Holly
Practical, perseverant, perfectionist, strong.

Hazel
Organized, analytical, perfectionist, academic.

Vine
Perceptive, kind, changeable, romantic, refined.

Ivy
Energetic, optimistic, extroverted, charismatic.

Reed
Inner strength, secretive, jealous, honorable.

Elder
Energetic, thrill and freedom seeker, extroverted.

Birch characteristics
Strong, hardworking, driven, resilient.

ROWAN
(January 22–Febuary 18)

CELTIC TREE ZODIAC

ASH
(February 19–March 17)

ALDER
(March 18–April 14)

WILLOW
(April 15–May 12)

HAWTHORN
(May 13–June 9)

OAK
(June 10–July 7)

HOLLY
(July 8–August 4)

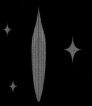

HAZEL
(August 5–September 1)

VINE
(September 2–September 29)

IVY
(September 30–October 27)

REED
(October 28–November 24)

ELDER
(November 25–December 23)

BIRCH
(December 24–January 21)

SALT & ITS *Properties*

Salt is considered one of the most sacred minerals the Earth produces and has a long connection with Witchcraft. It's used to represent the element of Earth on an altar or in elemental magick and many spells and rituals make use of it. Salt is mostly used for purification and cleansing. It is also used in protection, such as in circle casting, and can be used to banish and create barriers. Try and avoid using salt in outdoor spells and rituals as it kills any plant and insect life it touches. Crushed-up eggshells or sand are a great alternative.

TABLE SALT

Good for protection, cleansing, and purifying, table salt is affordable, easy to buy, and is a good addition to any Witch's cupboard. Table salt is a substitute for any other type of salt, so if this is the only kind of salt you have available, it will work in any spell. Salt is salt, regardless of its color or coarseness, and all salt has protective and cleansing properties.

SEA SALT

Whiter and coarser than table salt, sea salt is aligned with magick associated with the Water element but specifically to the ocean. It is a great addition to a cleansing ritual bath.

BLACK SALT

Made from salt mixed with charcoal or the black scrapings from your cauldron, black salt is highly protective and is used to absorb toxic energy, making it ideal to use in protection spells and for circle casting. Mix salt with your left-over incense or charcoal ashes for a quick recipe. If you're in the broom closet, but are able to burn incense sticks, black salt can be made in small batches for easy concealment.

HIMALAYAN PINK SALT

This salt gets its color from trace minerals such as calcium and magnesium. Its gentle energy is incredibly healing and can remove any negative block. Due to its pink color, it's used traditionally in love magick. It can help heal friendships, is a good addition to a self-love ritual, and can aid emotional healing. It can also remove love spells.

CELTIC SEA SALT

Light gray, celtic sea salt contains a little water, and can feel moist. It is considered the purest form of salt, which means it can be more effective at cleansing and purifying.

RED SALT

This unprocessed sea salt from Hawaii is mixed with volcanic red clay. Protective and cleansing, it's used in magick associated with love and lust.

TABLE SALT
Offers all-around protection
and purification.

SEA SALT
Associated with magick that
aligns to Water.

RED SALT
Associated with love and
lust magick.

SALT IN
WITCHCRAFT

CELTIC SEA SALT
Associated with cleansing
and purifying.

BLACK SALT
Highly protective.

HIMALAYAN PINK SALT
Great for love magick
and healing.

BENZOIN
Purifying, cleansing,
protection

COPAL
Grounding, protection,
love

MYRRH
Purifying, healing,
banishing

RESIN
AND GUM
PROPERTIES

DRAGON'S BLOOD
Love, cleansing,
protection

GUM ARABIC
Raises vibrations,
platonic love, protection

FRANKINCENSE
Purifying, consecration,
protection

RESINS
& Gums

Resins and gums are natural sticky substances from trees and plants, and are usually collected by tapping the tree or plant. Resins are not water soluble, whereas gums are. Both have heady scents and can be used in rituals and spells, burned as offerings, and used as a base incense ingredient.

BENZOIN *(Styrax benzoin)*

This resin is highly purifying and cleansing. Benzoin attracts good energy and keeps away negativity, so is an ideal addition to protective spells. It can be carried in a spell bag or sprinkled around your home for protection. It can also be burned to help with concentration and mental focus.

COPAL *(Bursera odorata)*

Copal resin is good at clearing stagnant energies from a room and its light scent turns negative energies into positive ones. Used in love magick, it can represent the heart in a poppet. It can be burned as a grounding, incense when meditating, and is a handy substitution for any resin or gum.

DRAGON'S BLOOD *(Daemonorops draco)*

This resin is used in love, cleansing, protection, and banishing magick. Burn as incense to cleanse a room of negativity. Grind into a powder and sprinkle it around your home and doorways for protection against outside influence.

FRANKINCENSE *(Boswellia carterii)*

Frankincense gum is aromatic and purifying when burned as incense. It's ideal for cleansing your sacred space and altar. When burned, frankincense can be used to consecrate magickal tools and objects—pass the item you want to consecrate through the smoke. Carry some frankincense in your pocket for protection.

GUM ARABIC *(Acacia senegal)*

This natural gum is used in protection spells and can help stimulate psychic abilities. Burned as incense, it can raise the vibrations in a space. It's used in love magick, but only for platonic love and friendships. Gum arabic (and all resins) can bind incense ingredients together—dissolve in a little hot water before adding other ingredients.

MYRRH *(Commiphora myrrha)*

This natural gum resin is cleansing and purifying when burned as incense. It can also be used with frankincense in banishing spells, and in reversing negative magick such as hexes. Myrrh can be used for healing and will increase the power of all ingredients mixed with it.

BLENDING YOUR OWN
Incense

You can make loose incense from a number of different ingredients. Resins, such as frankincense and copal, are commonly used for a base—they smolder and last for longer. Woods, such as sandalwood and cedar, are also another possible ingredient. Like resins and gums, woods make a good base and are usually mixed with them to make the incense last longer. Herbs are probably the most popular ingredients in loose incense, but they burn away quite quickly on their own—this is why herbs are generally mixed with a resin, gum, or wood.

The first step in making your incense is to choose the ingredients. Refer to the 'Herbs by Intention', (page 76) and 'Resins & Gums' (page 85) sections to help you choose ingredients that align with your intent—this is the most important point when putting your incense together because they must reflect and strengthen your particular purpose to help you manifest your chosen goal.

You can also choose your ingredients based on fragrance. All herbs, woods, and resins have their own particular note and picking what you want to use based on the different depths of fragrance is a way to make sure your incense smells amazing, and is also aligned to your intentions. As a rule, I've found that choosing at least two ingredients with base notes, two to three with middle notes and two to three with top notes works well, but be experimental and see what works best for you in terms of magickal properties as well as aroma.

BASE NOTES
Amber, benzoin, cedar, copal, dragon's blood, frankincense, juniper, myrrh, patchouli, sage, sandalwood, valerian, vanilla.

MIDDLE NOTES
Basil, chamomile, camphor, catnip, clove, hyssop, iris, mugwort, lavender, lemon balm, lemongrass rhubarb, rose, saffron, sweet grass, turmeric.

TOP NOTES
Bay, cardamom, cilantro, eucalyptus, ginger, hibiscus, marjoram, nutmeg, pine needles, rosemary, star anise, thyme.

Measure out each part of your ingredients by weight using a scale, or by volume using spoons and cups. Then, mix the ingredients together thoroughly. As you do, infuse the incense with your intentions. Focus on each ingredient's properties, how they can help you manifest your goals, and how you will feel when you do. When you're ready, heat a charcoal disc and place it in a heatproof holder. Give it a few minutes until it starts to turn white, and then sprinkle your incense over the top to release the aromas.

BLENDING YOUR OWN INCENSE

1. Choose ingredients that align to your intentions.

2. You can also choose ingredients based on fragrance.

4. Experiment with different blends to see what best works for you.

3. Mix your ingredients together thoroughly.

5. As you do, infuse your incense with your intentions to strengthen their properties.

6. Burn on a hot charcoal disc to release the aromas. Enjoy!

START

FINISH

METALS
& Their Properties

Many of us wear jewelry, but often it's the crystal or stone that is set into the metal that's the focus and why we choose to wear it at all. But metals shouldn't be overlooked! Just like herbs and resins, metals have their own different magickal properties and can be used in spells and rituals like any other ingredient.

Using metals in magick isn't spoken about as much as it should be—it's not just the green gifts the Earth produces that can be effectively used in magick. Everything on Earth possesses its own energy, which can add power to a spell or ritual, and metal is no different. It's also a very subtle way of wearing your Craft if you are practicing from the broom closet. A piece of jewelry in a corresponding metal can be worn to support your intentions for the day.

Here are the most-used metals in Witchcraft and their magickal properties and uses.

GOLD

Aligned with the energies of the Sun, gold is associated with wealth and abundance. It can be used as a money charm to attract prosperity. Gold amplifies any other crystals or stones that are put with it. White gold combines the energy of the Sun and Moon and amplifies the energies of crystals or stones that are placed with it.

SILVER

Connected to the energies of the Moon and the element Water, silver has feminine energies. It is aligned to magick associated with psychic abilities, wisdom, and intuition, and is used to increase divinatory powers. It is also connected to the spirit realm and the Goddess Selene. Wear amethyst set in a piece of silver jewelry during divination to give your abilities a boost or wear moonstone in silver to connect to the cycles of the Moon.

COPPER

This metal aligns with Venus and is associated with love, balance, prosperity, and beauty. It also has many healing properties, which is why copper bracelets are often worn. Copper can be used to wire-wrap crystals and can be used in spells and rituals. Wear a copper wire-wrapped piece of rose quartz to attract love into your life or a piece of wire-wrapped clear quartz for balance. Use copper coins in money and prosperity magick.

METALS AND
THEIR PROPERTIES

GOLD

The Sun
Wealth
Abundance
Prosperity
Amplifies energy

The Moon
Psychic abilities
Wisdom
Intuition
Divination

SILVER

COPPER

Venus
Love
Balance
Prosperity
Beauty

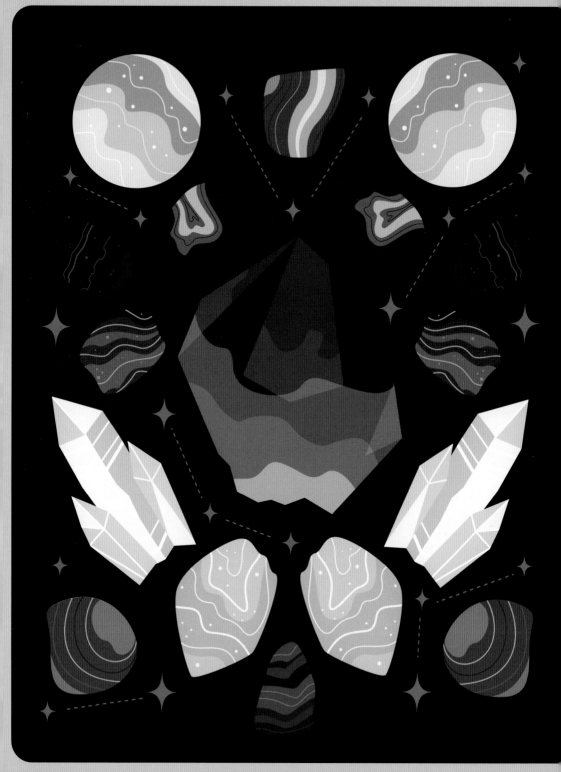

5

CRYSTALS

With their beautiful colors and extraordinary shapes, crystals have long been a source of fascination for humans. They are associated with the element Earth and working with them can deepen your relationship with the natural world as you connect to the very energies of the ground beneath your feet.

Formed deep within the earth over thousands of years, each type of crystal has its own specific energy. Choosing the right crystals for your spell or ritual can help to channel energy and aid your magick.

Working with crystals isn't essential, so you are no less a Witch if you don't feel called to include them in your practice. But if you want to start your own collection, this chapter includes the 16 most popular crystals used in Witchcraft, the elements they are associated with, their magickal properties, and how to use them.

When buying crystals, the good news is they are often inexpensive, but it's important to know where your crystals come from, so I'll raise a few ethical points to think about before your next purchase. If you are using crystals in your practice, they must also be cared for properly in order to get the very best from them. In this chapter, I will show you how to do this, from cleansing to charging, to which crystals are water and Sun safe as well as choosing the right-shaped crystal for your workings.

CRYSTAL *Grimoire*

AMAZONITE *(Earth)*

This crystal gets its name from the Amazon River, the place where this crystal was first found. It's a soothing blue, green, and white stone known for its ability to bring calm and peace. It's perfect to hold during meditation if you need to ground and center yourself or balance any unsteady emotions. Amazonite is also the ideal stone to carry if you're feeling stressed or agitated. Often called the stone of courage, amazonite can help to increase your sense of confidence—it is a good crystal to carry if you're feeling unsure of yourself. It also activates the throat and heart chakras, aiding and strengthening communication.

AMETHYST *(Water)*

A type of quartz known for its powerfully protective qualities, amethyst absorbs negative energy. Carry or wear it as jewelry for personal protection or place it inside, near your front door, for home protection. Amethyst can calm, soothe, and bring peace, making it a great crystal to meditate with as well as use in magick relating to sleep, anxiety, stress, and well-being. It also activates psychic abilities and is a good stone to use during divination. Amethyst opens the third eye, allowing a heightened sense of awareness and intuition. To activate this, keep a piece of amethyst under your pillow or on top of a dream journal, or lay down and meditate with a piece on your forehead. It also encourages psychic dreams.

AVENTURINE *(Air)*

A microcrystalline quartz that is usually green in color, aventurine is known for its ability to manifest prosperity and wealth, and attract luck. Carry aventurine as a lucky charm to draw abundance. Aventurine can spark creativity and is ideal to wear when working on any creative project. It can also encourage a more positive mindset. It balances emotions, calms anger, and brings stability—it also opens the heart chakra. This can promote gratitude and feelings of compassion. Wear aventurine as jewelry, carry in your pocket, or use during meditation.

BLACK TOURMALINE *(Earth)*

This powerful crystal is great to add to any protective spell bags or carry for physical and psychic protection. It will protect you from negative entities and those things that sap your energy. It's a good addition to any grounding ritual. Black tourmaline can bring about a sense of balance and stability so is ideal to meditate with or carry in your pocket. This crystal is very cleansing, can be used to clear unwanted energies from your aura, and cleanse other crystals.

CRYSTAL GRIMOIRE

1. Amazonite—Calm, peace, courage, confidence
2. Amethyst—Protection, psychic abilities, dreams, calm
3. Aventurine—Prosperity, luck, creativity, balancing emotions
4. Black Tourmaline—Protection, psychic ability, grounding, cleansing

CRYSTAL GRIMOIRE

1. Carnelian—Prosperity, courage, protection, success
2. Citrine—Joy, optimism, abundance, manifestation
3. Clear Quartz—Amplifies, psychic abilities, balance, healing
4. Fluorite—Protection, grounding, stabilizing, psychic abilites

CARNELIAN *(Earth & Fire)*

A reddish-brown kind of chalcedony, carnelian is a member of the quartz family. It attracts prosperity and can be carried as a talisman to bring success in money-related issues. A stone of action, carnelian can promote courage, passion, motivation, and inspiration. Use it in a spell bag or wear it when you work on creative projects to fire up your energy. Carnelian is also protective, particularly in the astral plane. Use it during astral travel for protection and to enhance your second sight. It can also help you find any hidden talents or abilities.

CITRINE *(Fire)*

This form of yellow quartz brings a sense of warmth, joy, happiness, and all-around good vibes. Its sunny energy can boost self-confidence and build up a feeling of self-worth so is ideal to wear in jewelry or carry with you throughout the day. Citrine stimulates optimism, willpower, vitality, and attracts prosperity and abundance. Carry a piece in your wallet to attract wealth. Citrine is the stone of manifestation and can help you to actualize your goals. It can also protect you from nightmares when placed under your pillow.

CLEAR QUARTZ *(Fire & Water)*

This natural conductor of energy is associated with enhancing psychic abilities. Use it during divination to give you clearer sight. Known as the "master healer," wearing clear quartz can help the immune system, regulate your inner energy flow, and bring a sense of balance. It can also help to bring clarity and expand consciousness. Clear quartz also amplifies the properties of the crystals it is put with, so the next time you are working with crystals, add some clear quartz for a boost of energy by placing them on your altar or wearing as jewelry.

FLUORITE *(Air)*

This common mineral comes in green, blue, and purple. It purifies the mind and helps to bring clarity and order. Place a piece of fluorite on your desk at work or where you are studying to bring orderliness and structure to what you do. Fluorite is a highly protective and stabilizing stone and is ideal to use for grounding. It absorbs any negative energy from its surroundings and heightens psychic abilities. It can also be placed under your pillow to protect you from negativity as you sleep and helps you find solutions in your dreams.

HEMATITE *(Earth)*

A black and silver, opaque, semiprecious crystal, hematite can help to ground and balance as well as help us find our center. It can bring stability as it activates the root chakra and anchors us to nature. Hematite absorbs any negative emotions surrounding it and can reduce feelings of stress, worry, or anxiety and can make you feel more self-assured. It's also protective and is a good stone to carry with you because it soaks up any electromagnetic energy and dissipates it. Hematite can help you focus your mind and assist with logical thinking—it is a great crystal for students or anyone working on a project because it enhances concentration and imagination.

LABRADORITE *(Water & Air)*

When this dark stone is moved, it shows an iridescent rainbow of green, yellow, blue, and red. It is associated with spiritual transformation, and helps you access higher realms of consciousness as well as enhancing visions. It helps us tap into our natural intuitive abilities and enhances them. Hold it or wear it as jewelry during divination or when you want to tap into your higher self. Labradorite is also a highly protective stone and helps to deflect negative energy by creating a shielding force. It's a good stone to banish fears and insecurities—use a tumbled Labradorite crystal when you meditate to help release any uneasiness or worry.

MOONSTONE *(Water)*

This translucent white crystal has a sheen when moved. Since this stone is connected to the Moon, it is also connected to intuition and enhancing psychic abilities. Meditating with moonstone can bring a sense of calm because it balances the chakras and heightens awareness. Moonstone has a feminine energy and is a reminder that we, like the Moon, flow through cycles. It connects us to the energy of the Earth and other natural cycles taking place around us within nature. It's a wonderful stone to take on a nature walk as you see the part of the cycle or season the Earth is currently in. Moonstone is a reminder that the world is in constant change, which is the circle of life.

RED JASPER *(Fire)*

This gentle stone can nurture and sustain us through difficult times. It can ease stress and encourage tranquillity. It's a great accompaniment to any self-care ritual as it offers support and encourages a sense of wholeness. Red jasper facilitates healing on an emotional level by bringing calm and balance to the body. If you are struggling to find control of your emotions, this is the stone to keep with you to gently help you find your center again. Red Jasper is protective, and it absorbs any negative energy from the environment around it. It's an ideal crystal to use as a protective talisman and can be used to correct any injustices.

CRYSTAL GRIMOIRE

1. Hematite—Protection, concentration, stabilizing, balance
2. Labradorite—Protection, banishes fear, transformation, intuition
3. Moonstone—Intuition, psychic abilities, cycles, balance
4. Red Jasper—Strength, courage, tranquality, protection

ROSE QUARTZ *(Earth)*

With its delicate pink tone, rose quartz is possibly the most instantly recognizable crystal. It's the stone of love that opens the heart chakra so we can both give love and receive it. Rose quartz helps to attract love, and wearing it can help give an appreciation of the beauty around you. It is the perfect stone to include in any self-love ritual. Place a few tumbled stones in a jar of clean water for 24 hours, then sip throughout the day to open yourself up to its loving energies. Rose quartz can also help release old issues and facilitate forgiveness, so it is a good stone for meditation.

SELENITE *(Water)*

This translucent white crystal has fluid energy used for cleansing and clearing away any negative energy. It's a great crystal to use to cleanse and charge other crystals —simply place the crystals you want to charge either on or near a piece of selenite for 24 hours. Selenite is associated with spirituality and wisdom as it opens the crown and third eye chakras. Meditating with a piece of selenite on either of these chakras will raise intuition levels and expand awareness. It is excellent at unblocking stagnant energy and gets it flowing again.

SMOKY QUARTZ *(Earth)*

This brownish-colored crystal dispels fear and is one of the best stones for grounding and for connecting with the element Earth. It can calm anxiety and elevate your mood. Keep a piece of smoky quartz nearby to help you during times of stress. It can also help to focus your concentration and regain mental clarity and sight. Smoky quartz transmutes any negative energy in its environment into positive energy and is a strongly protective stone. It gives psychic protection so is a good crystal to wear during spirit work. Smoky quartz can also be used to help us leave those things in the past that no longer serve our highest good. Let it help you let go by keeping a piece near to you to facilitate the process.

SODALITE *(Water)*

A blue crystal, sodalite usually has veins of white running through it. It works to deepen and develop your sense of intuition and make your mind sharper and more logical. This can be beneficial when used in divination as it can help you see patterns in the cards you didn't notice before. Sodalite aids clear communication and helps you to express yourself and your emotions so others can understand. It's a great companion for those who engage in public speaking because it calms emotions and boosts communication skills. It's soothing energy can bring a feeling of calm to quell anxiety and it is a good crystal to stabilize your energy. Carry sodalite in your pocket, or as jewelry worn against your skin to bring peace.

CRYSTAL GRIMOIRE

1. Rose Quartz—Love, beauty, releases issues, self-love
2. Selenite—Cleansing, charging, wisdom, intuition
3. Sodalite—Intuition, communication, calm, sharpens mind
4. Smoky Quartz—Grounding, protection, mental clarity, dispels fear

CLEANSING
& Charging

All crystals need to be prepared—cleansed and charged—properly before using, particularly new crystals you haven't worked with before.

CLEANSING

Cleansing crystals removes any unwanted or negative energies that have become attached to them and prepares them for use. This should be done regularly and can be done in several ways, sometimes harnessing the energy of the elements.

SOIL *(Earth)*
Bury your crystals in the ground for 24 hours to use the power of Mother Earth. This method is slow and gentle.

VISUALIZATION *(Air)*
Visualize a bright white light that moves from the bottom to the top of your crystal, pushing out the darkness of any negative energies.

SMOKE *(Fire)*
Burn cleansing herbs such as rosemary and lavender, then pass your crystals through the smoke. Combining Air, Fire, and Earth, makes this a powerful cleansing method.

WATER *(Water)*
Run Sun safe crystals under water. See page 102 for a list of water safe and unsafe crystals. For crystals that aren't water safe, place them near a glass of water for 24 hours to cleanse instead.

CHARGING

Crystals gradually lose energy. Charging restores lost energy and raises the vibration of the crystal to amplify its magickal properties.

SALT *(Earth)*
Check your crystal is salt safe and then place it on a bed of natural salt for 24 hours to recharge and replenish it's energy. Dispose of the salt by throwing it in the bin.

MOONLIGHT *(Air)*
Place your crystals in the light of the full Moon overnight outside or on a windowsill to charge.

SUNLIGHT *(Fire)*
The Sun can be used to charge crystals, although not all crystals are Sun safe. See page 105 for crystals damaged by sunlight.

SELENITE *(Water)*
To use the power and energies of Water, place smaller crystals on a slab of selenite to charge for 24 hours.

CLEANSING AND CHARGING

Cleansing crystals removes any unwanted or negative energies that's accumulated through use.

This removes energy blockages so the energy can flow. This makes the crystal more effective in spells and rituals.

The four elements can be used to cleanse crystals: soil, smoke, water, and sound.

The energy of any crystal is not unlimited—over time it loses energy through use.

Charging replenishes this energy and raises the vibrational energy of a crystal to activate its energy.

The power of four elements can also be used to charge: sunlight, moonlight, salt, and selenite.

CRYSTALS *& Water*

One of the easiest ways to cleanse crystals is by running them under flowing water, but not all crystals are water safe. Many crystals can be damaged when they encounter water and I've certainly ruined one or two crystals over the years before I knew this. Water can damage crystals in several ways, depending upon the chemical composition of each crystal. It can cause them to dull and lose their shine, start to break down, and, in some cases, can make them dissolve.

The hardness of the crystal usually determines whether it will be damaged by water. Hardness is measured on the Mohs Hardness Scale invented in 1822, where each crystal is given a number 1–10 based on its mineral and metal content, which then determines how hard or soft the crystal is. The higher the number, the harder the crystal. This is relevant when looking at crystals and how they react when put in water because the softer the crystal, the less tolerant to water it is and the more likely it will get damaged.

Those crystals that have a score of 5 and upward are generally water safe; those below this will be damaged in some way by contact with water. There are some exceptions to this. Although crystals such as pyrite and hematite are hard, because they contain iron ore, they will rust and go dull when placed in water for too long. Some crystals also leech toxic metals into the water—this not only gradually damages the crystals, but they must not be placed in water you plan to consume.

Amazonite, although it has a hardness of 6–7 on the Mohs scale, is not water safe as it contains copper, which turns the water toxic. Always do your research before using water with any crystals to make sure they're water safe.

Here is a list of the water safe and water unsafe crystals. I've placed crystals such as amazonite on the unsafe list because, although they may be hard enough to not be damaged by water, they contain metal that make the water they're in toxic.

WATER SAFE

Agate, amethyst, ametrine, aventurine, beryl, bloodstone, carnelian, chalcedony, citrine, clear, rose and smoky quartz, diamond, emerald, garnet, jasper, obsidian, topaz, tiger's eye.

NOT WATER SAFE

Amazonite, amber, angelite, aquamarine, azurite, black and blue tourmaline, calcite, chrysocolla, fluorite, gypsum, hematite, jade, jet, kunzite, kyanite, labradorite, lapis lazuli, lepidolite, malachite, moonstone, opal, pyrite, rhodochrosite, sodalite, selenite, sugilite, spinel, tangerine quartz, turquoise.

CRYSTALS AND WATER

Not all crystals are water safe, so it's always good to research first.

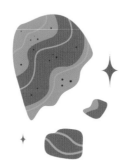

Some crystals can go dull or even start to dissolve on contact with water.

Some crystals are not water safe as they give off toxic metals that leech into the water.

Softer crystals like selenite are not water safe.

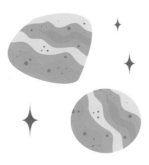

As a rule, those crystals that end in "ite", like amazonite, are not water safe.

For crystals that are not water safe, place them next to a glass of water to cleanse them.

CRYSTALS AND SUNLIGHT

Direct sunlight damages some crystals and makes them fade and become brittle.

Generally, transparent and semi-transparent crystals such as amethyst are more prone to fade in sunlight.

Fire stones such as carnelian, red chalcedony, red jasper, and sunstone are generally Sun safe.

Faded crystals generally still have the same magickal properties as they did before they faded.

Doing your research is crucial before charging your crystals in the sunlight so that you can prevent damage.

It's a good idea to keep your photosensitive crystals wrapped in a soft cloth and out of direct sunlight.

CRYSTALS & Sunlight

Sunlight is a wonderful way to cleanse and charge crystals, but some will fade if placed in sunlight for too long. Although you might think that sunlight won't fade a crystal if it spends 10 minutes here and there in the Sun, over time, this will affect the pigments of color. Citrine, for example, can fade to clear after spending just four hours in the Sun and fluorite can become very hot after just 15 minutes of Sun exposure.

As a loose and general rule, transparent and semi-transparent crystals such as amethyst and fluorite tend to be more sensitive to light than opaque crystals. Sunlight doesn't just have the power to fade certain crystals—it can make them more prone to damage, and in extreme situations, can cause them to break down. Even clear quartz can start to go brittle and get tiny cracks in its surface after only two to three hours in the Sun.

Some crystals will fade naturally overtime, but time spent in the sunlight will accelerate this process. The good thing is, I've found that although their color may have faded, it doesn't affect the energy of the crystal or its magickal properties. Unfortunately, I've discovered this the hard way. Overexposure to the Sun has faded my favorite piece of amethyst so the purple color isn't as vivid, but it has not changed its energy or made it less powerful or effective. If you have faded crystals in your collection, don't be afraid to use them and work with their energies in your practice.

As a rule, fire-colored crystals such as carnelian and sunstone enjoy time in the Sun and are Sun safe, but always do your research when using a new or unfamiliar crystal in the Sun, to avoid damage. Try keeping your photosensitive crystals wrapped in a soft cloth to shield them from any unnecessary light.

SUN SAFE CRYSTALS

Black obsidian, black onyx, carnelian, howlite, labradorite, lapis lazuli, malachite, moonstone, red chalcedony, red jasper, sunstone, tourmaline.

NOT SUN SAFE

Amethyst, ametrine, apatite, aquamarine, aventurine, beryl, calcite, celestite, citrine, fluorite, jade, kunzite, opal, sapphire, smoky quartz, sodalite, spirit quartz, super seven, topaz, turquoise.

ENERGIES OF DIFFERENT
Shaped Crystals

Some crystals are formed naturally, and some are carved by human hands, but the shape of a crystal has an impact on its energy and how it is channelled. Although the shape of the crystal is important, it doesn't give a crystal more power or energy, but it does mean you will experience its energy differently. This means that certain shapes are better suited to specific kinds of magickal workings.

TUMBLED CRYSTALS

They give a gentle, balanced energy and can be used in any kind of workings. They are affordable, practical, and perfect for keeping in your pocket. Don't be fooled by their size—they still pack an energetic punch.

RAW CRYSTALS

These are crystals in their natural form and have irregular energy. They come in all shapes and sizes and their surface is rough. They can feel more powerful because they have come from Mother Earth in their untouched form.

SPHERE

These are perfectly rounded, highly polished balls associated with divination, specifically scrying. They bring an even energy as they radiate their power in all directions. Their calming energy makes them great for meditation.

CRYSTAL POINTS

These concentrate and direct energy though their points, amplifying energy that can help when intention setting. They can be used to raise the vibration of a space.

PYRAMID

By anchoring your intentions through its solid base, then strengthening them though the point, a pyramid assists manifestation, sending it into the universe in a concentrated beam. Write your intentions on a piece of paper and place under a crystal pyramid to speed up manifestation.

CRYSTAL CLUSTERS

These multiple crystal points contain strong vibrational energy that radiates in all different directions, making them good amplifiers of energy. Clusters are great space room cleansers because their energy reaches out into every part of the room.

DOUBLE TERMINATED CRYSTALS

These crystals are able to transmit and receive energy at the same time. This makes them good for use in crystal grids because they can move energy. Their balanced energy is useful if you've lost your equilibrium.

ENERGIES OF DIFFERENT SHAPED CRYSTALS

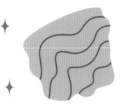

RAW CRYSTALS
Irregular energy
Natural form
Rough surfaces

TUMBLED CRYSTALS
Even energy
Smooth surfaces
Useful in any spell

SPHERE
Even, balanced energy
Rough and polished
Good for meditation
and scrying

CRYSTAL POINTS
Concentrates and
directs energy
Amplifies and raises
energy

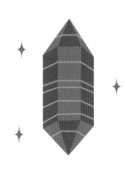

PYRAMID
Focused energy
Aids manifestation

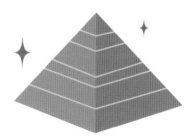

DOUBLE TERMINATED
Transmits and
recieves energy
Balances
Can move energy
Good in crystal grids

CLUSTERS
Radiates energy everywhere
Strong vibrations
Amplifies energy

CRYSTALS AND ELIXIRS

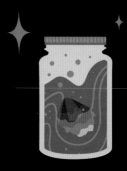

An elixir is crystal-infused water, often preserved with alcohol.

Elixirs go by many names, but they all mean the same thing. They can be made using two methods.

The direct method involves putting your chosen crystal directly into water to infuse.

The indirect method involves placing crystals around a jar of water to project their energy into the water.

You MUST make sure the crystals you use in water and plan to consume are safe and non-toxic.

The different varieties of quartz such as citrine are safe and non-toxic and are commonly used to make elixir.

CRYSTALS
& Elixirs

The healing and magickal powers of crystals can be harnessed in an elixir. Sometimes known as gem water or crystal essences, elixirs are crystal-infused water, often with alcohol to preserve it. They are nature's cocktails and making them can really help you to connect to the Water and Earth elements. You can make herbal elixirs in the same way. Elixirs are usually made using either a direct and indirect method.

DIRECT

This places crystals directly into clean drinking water. Over time, the energy of the crystals will permeate the water with their specific vibrations as they project their energy. When we consume the water, we absorb the benefits of this energy in a concentrated form. Only choose crystals that are safe (see page 105). Many different varieties of quartz (amethyst, citrine, rose, clear, and smoky) are used because they are safe and non-toxic.

Directly cleanse your crystals

1. Choose and cleanse your safe crystals, then place into a jar of clean drinking water.
2. Ground and center yourself as you connect with the crystals, their energy, and your intentions.
3. Cover your jar with a cloth to protect the crystals and then place it in the sunlight (if your crystals are Sun safe) or moonlight (if using crystals such as citrine, which aren't Sun safe) for three to four hours. Other Witches may leave it for longer, such as 12 or 24 hours. Do what feels right to you.
4. Refrigerate and sip the water throughout the day.
5. Without alcohol, your elixir will only last for a day or so. Add 50% vodka or brandy, glycerol, or vinegar if you want to keep it for more than a week. This is optional, and you must use and consume it sensibly.
6. If you add a preservative, you can make a dosage bottle. Use a dark stopper bottle to protect it from the Sun and for ease of use. Put three to four drops in your tea, in your bath, dropped directly onto the tongue, added to essential oils, or to a room spray.

INDIRECT

You can also make elixirs without exposing the crystal to water. This allows you to make use of those crystals that leech toxic metals into the water. As crystals project their energy outward, simply place your chosen crystals next to a covered glass or jar of water and allow the crystals to infuse the water with their beneficial energies for the same length of time as the direct method. Consume your elixir as explained above.

PROGRAMMING *Crystals*

Crystals are sensitive and pick up the vibrational energies of their surroundings, be it good or bad. That's why cleansing is so important, so we can remove any unwanted or negative energies before we use them for magickal or healing purposes. The process of programming is built upon the belief that crystals have a natural ability to absorb energy from their surroundings and we can use it to help set and strengthen our intentions.

Programming is a way of communicating with your crystal and telling it exactly what you want it to help you with. It's a way of aiding manifestation because you are magnifying your intent and calling upon a specific quality the crystal embodies to help you. For example, you could program a piece of rose quartz if your wanted to foster feelings of self-love or program a piece of amethyst if you wanted to increase your psychic abilities. Programming is a way of tuning into the crystal itself and using one of the qualities it embodies to help you reach your goals.

It's not necessary to program a crystal for it to work. Some Witches program all their crystals, others only program specific ones for special purposes and some Witches don't feel the need to program any. Do what feels right to you. I'll share with you how I program my crystals, but feel free to modify it to suit your needs and style. Like with most things in my Craft, I like to keep things simple—all you need is the power of your intent!

Once you've chosen the crystal that aligns best with your intentions, sit somewhere comfy where you won't be disturbed and hold it in your hands for a moment. When you're ready, visualize a pure white light slowly filling up the crystal. This is the light of your intention. In your head or out loud, state your intention. Be as specific as you can. For example, if you want to program a piece of rose quartz to attract love, be as specific as you can about the kind of love you want to attract. Is it romantic or platonic? How do you want the crystal to specifically help you manifest this?

When you have told the crystal what you want, sit in its presence for a while, visualizing the last part of the crystal filling up with the white light. Sit as long as you feel you need to until the whole crystal is glowing with light. Choosing a smaller stone to program is good because you can put it in a pouch and carry it with you as a reminder to strengthen your intention and do the mundane things that will bring you closer to your goals. When you no longer need the crystal for this purpose, simply cleanse it, to be used again for another purpose.

PROGRAMMING CRYSTALS

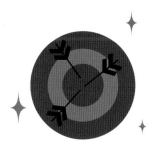

Programming a crystal is a way of communication whereby you fill it with your intention.

You tell the crystal what you want help with as you call upon its qualities to help you achieve your goals.

Not all Witches program their crystals so it's up to you if it feels right to incorporate it into your Craft.

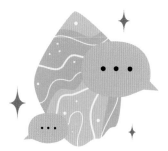

Programming a crystal aids manifestation because it strengthens and amplifies your intentions.

To program a crystal, pick one that aligns with your intentions and hold it in your hands, visualizing it filling up with white light.

As you do, speak about your specific intentions and how the crystal can help you to achieve them.

CRYSTALS AND ETHICS

It's good to know about the origins of the crystals we buy.

Some crystals are mined illegally and damage the Mother Earth as her treasures are plundered.

Other crystals are mined by exploiting child labor or are known to fund terrorism.

Crystals are used for their energy so make sure they are not tainted by the bad energy of this practice.

Do your research about the sellers and stores that sell ethically sourced crystals before you buy.

Ask the sellers or stores where their crystals are sourced from and if they can't answer, consider purchasing from somewhere that can.

CRYSTALS
& Ethics

Many Witches incorporate the use of crystals somewhere into their Craft, whether it's using them in spells and rituals, on altars, for healing, or wearing crystal jewelry. But it's important to know where our crystals come from—their colorful and shiny facades can often hide a dark side that few people think about. Many crystals have unfortunately come from places in the world where illegal mining occurs, and the Earth is being damaged as she is stripped of all her natural treasures.

Crystals are used for healing and magickal workings, but if they are ripped from the earth in such a destructive way, the energy of these crystals will be tainted to say the least, and no amount of cleansing will be able to completely clear them. The energies they bring will not necessarily be pure because the circumstances surrounding how they were mined involved so much destruction of the Earth. Witches work in respectful harmony and balance with nature and using these kinds of crystals works against the very core of Witchcraft.

Crystal mining is also responsible for funding bloody conflicts around the world. Lapis lazuli mines located in Afghanistan are known to provide the Taliban with millions of dollars each year that goes to fund terrorist activity around the world. Unfortunately, there is an even darker side to crystal mining as many illegal mines use child labor. Thousands of children as young as seven are known to work in industrial conditions in places such as the Democratic Republic of the Congo, Brazil, and Madagascar. These countries' destructive, illegal mining practices not only damage the Earth, but also young lives.

When buying crystals, it's vital to do your research to see which stores or sellers can tell you about where the crystals were mined. There's a good chance that if a seller can't provide you with the name of the country from where a crystal was mined, then they sell crystals that come from a dubious source, particularly if the crystals are quite a lot cheaper than other stores. Luckily, more sellers are able to provide this information and I would certainly recommend taking the time to find out before your next purchase.

6
DIVINATION

It's an enduring stereotypical view of the Witch—an old woman with long grey hair bent over staring intently into a crystal ball. Witches are not just old women and can be a person of any gender or age, but the one thing that unites many Witches is the use of divination—the practice of bringing what is unseen into the light—into their Craft.

Divination is the art of finding hidden knowledge and using tools such as crystals balls to uncover this information. It can be used to access your higher self, and it's from here that answers can be found. Generally, the answers to your questions are not presented in a simple yes or no form (except when using a pendulum) but are given in the form of guidance. It is up to us to interpret it using a divinatory tool of your choice.

Divination is not something that should be pushed, and it doesn't make your Craft less valid if you choose not to practice it. Follow your intuition and do what feels right to you.

In this chapter, I want to explore a wide range of different divination methods, so you have the information to be able to see other practices that resonate. I will cover how to use runes, divination dice, and oracle cards as well as how to care for your divination tools so you can get the very best from them in readings.

WHAT ARE *Runes?*

Runes are the alphabet systems used by ancient Germanic and Nordic tribes of northern Europe, Scandinavia, and Britian. Where the symbols in the Latin alphabet are called "letters," the symbols in Germanic alphabets are referred to as "runes" and each has its own spiritual meanings. To make runes, the runic alphabet is drawn on pieces of stone, but they can be made from any material, including wood, crystal, metal, or even bone. I have made my own set using salt dough (you can find the recipe easily online) and I was very pleased with the results. They were easy and inexpensive to make, so it's a good option if you're a Witch on a budget.

Runes are better at hinting at answers rather than providing direct advice. They guide you through your issues by helping you see the bigger picture, the possibilities, and the variables at play. They will then leave you to figure out the finer details for yourself. Runes can give deep insights, but as with all forms of divination, the more you practice and connect with your runes and your own intuition, the more detailed your readings will become. To fully master working with runes takes a long time, so don't be discouraged if you find interpreting their meanings difficult at first. Keep going!

Like other forms of divination, runes don't give guidance that relate to established future events because the future is not fixed. You have the power to change the future if a reading tells you something about the future you don't like. You remain in the driving seat where you have the power to change your direction or follow a different route at any point. Runes help you to look at the possible causes and effects of the situation you are divining for, so that you can figure out what to do next.

The Germanic runic alphabets called The Elder Futhark and The Younger Futhark are the oldest and most common runic alphabets used today. The Elder Futhark consists of 24 runes divided into three groups of eight, known as an aett. Each aett is dedicated to a different deity—the first is to the Goddess Freya, with the first six runes spelling out the word "futhark." The second aett is dedicated to the God Heimdall and the third to the God Tyr. The Younger Futhark is a reduced version of the Elder and consists of 16 runes. They can be divided into two different styles, either the "long branch" or "short twig."

ELDER FUTHARK RUNES

Fehu
(F)
Wealth

Uruz
(U)
Strength

Thurisaz
(Th)
Danger

Ansuz
(A)
Prosperity

Raidho
(R)
Journey

Kaunan
(K)
Mortality

Gebo
(G)
Generosity

Wunjo
(W)
Blessings

Hagaiaz
(H)
Destruction

Naudhiz
(N)
Desire

Isaz
(I)
Deception

Jera
(J)
Reward

Eihwaz
(Ae)
Stability

Perthro
(P)
Destiny

Elhaz
(Z)
Protection

Sowilo
(S)
Success

Tiwaz
(T)
Justice

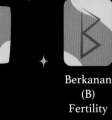
Berkanan
(B)
Fertility

Ehwaz
(E)
Trust

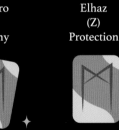
Mannaz
(M)
Support

Laguz
(L)
Chaos

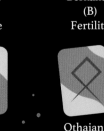
Ingwaz
(Hg)
Potential

Othaian
(O)
Heritage

Dagaz
(D)
Hope

FRAYA'S AET

HEIMDALL'S
AETT

TYR'S AETT

HOW TO
Use Runes

The word "rune" means "secret whisper," which gives an indication of their magickal and divinatory powers. To use as a form of divination, place all your runes in a pouch and as you ask a question, pull a rune from the bag and interpret its message. If you are a beginner, pulling one rune each day is a good way to learn more about their meanings.

You can also choose to carefully throw all your runes out onto a rune cloth or board, and you can then interpret them not only by their meaning but by their position on the cloth and their connection to those runes that have landed nearby. You can design your own rune cloth. For example, you might draw two circles on your cloth, one bigger and the other much smaller (placed inside the bigger circle). You could consider any runes that fall inside the smaller circle as events or guidance related to the present, the runes that fall outside both circles as guidance as relevant to a longer period of time, and those runes that fall in between the circles as counsel related to the near future.

Some runes boards include runes drawn onto them, whilst others don't. For those that do, you can throw blank stones or crystals onto the board to see which rune symbol they land closest to if you don't have any rune stones. If you don't have any rune stones and want to use a runes cloth that doesn't have runes drawn onto it either, you can just use small objects at your disposal to represent each of the 24 runes, and throw them onto the board. This could be a small piece of jewelry, like a ring pendant, coin, or crystal, just as long as you remember which item corresponds with which rune. These items can then be used as runes and cast onto the board.

Tarot cards can be used in specific spreads where each card position has a specific meaning (like the Celtic Cross), and runes can be used in a similar way. The Runic Cross is a traditional rune spread that can be used to gain a deeper insight into any situation or issue. The three-rune layout representing the past, present, and future is another popular spread, and so are the layouts using five and nine runes.

Runes can be used more widely in Witchcraft. They can be used as charms and talismans, can be added to spell bags and bottles, or can be carried to help you manifest what the rune represents. Choosing the runes that align with the intentions of your working is a simple but powerful way to reinforce these intentions and give a boost of energy to your spell. Using runes in your Craft can be incorporated into many kinds of workings, such as candle magick. For example, you could carve the rune Elhaz, (a protection rune) into a black candle, then light it for a simple protection spell. Runes are certainly very useful tools to have.

ORACLE *Cards*

Oracle cards have become a popular form of divination in recent years. They are great if you are just starting to practice divination but don't know where to begin. They are considered a little easier to read and less intimidating than tarot because they rely heavily on the imagery of each card to convey their message rather than having specific set meanings. It's not necessary to memorize the meaning of each deck, because every deck is different, but rather use your intuition to look at the images on the cards you pull and let them tell you what they mean.

The word oracle, meaning something that gives a prediction and reveals knowledge from a divine source, helps us understand why oracle cards are ideal to use for self-reflection and introspection. Whereas the Hermit tarot card will always mean the same in every deck regardless of how the artist has depicted it, oracle cards, due to their free-flowing and less structured nature, can mean something slightly different each time, depending on the situation and what your intuition sees. This brings more freedom to interpret the different images in your own way.

Oracle cards can be a welcomed addition to tarot spreads to give another layer of understanding to your reading. I often pull one oracle card for every tarot card in the spread I'm using to help me appreciate both the message of the tarot card on a deeper level and the message it is trying to convey. A good practice is to pull an oracle card at the start of each day and reflect on what it might mean—it will not only help you get more familiar with each card but will help you connect with your deck.

To help explain what oracle cards are and what they are used for, it's helpful to compare them with the most popular form of divination— tarot. Using oracle cards are a form of cartomancy (divination using a deck of cards) like tarot, but this is where the similarities between tarot and oracle ends.

Unlike tarot, oracle decks don't have a set number of cards in a deck. An oracle deck can have any number of cards, which is decided on by the creator of each deck. Many of the oracle decks on sale now have anything from 20 to 90 cards in a deck. Similarly, where a tarot deck is split into four suits—Wands, Swords, Pentacles, and Cups—an oracle deck doesn't follow this pattern and follows their own themes, decided on by each deck's creator. Some of my favorite oracle decks are based around astrology, animals, self-care, and the Moon. You could even make your own oracle cards based on something that calls to you. This is a great option for a creative Witch on a budget and could be a way of practicing divination while in the broom closet, if you are able to do it discreetly.

ORACLE CARDS

- All oracle decks are different and don't follow a structure like a tarot deck.
  - A deck can have any number of cards and follows its own themes.
  - Oracle decks rely heavily on the images on each card to convey their message.
- Oracle cards are a good place to start your divination journey as they are less intimidating than tarot.
  - They are fantastic tools for self-reflection and inner work, healing, and growth.
- Look at what is available and choose a deck with art that speaks to you. Or, make your own!

DIVINATION DICE

Astragalomancy is divination by use of dice. It is an ancient form of divination and is still used by many Witches, Pagans, and astrologers today. The oldest-known dice date from 5,000 years ago in modern-day Iran. One of the most common forms of dice divination used today uses three dice: one covered with planetary symbols, another with the signs of the zodiac, and the last covered with numbers.

It might look a little complicated at first but once you've done a few readings for yourself, you'll see it's pretty straightforward. If you're interested in giving this form of divination a try, a set of three dice can be bought inexpensively online. You can also write each sign and number on a separate piece of paper and put them in three separate bags. To use them for divination, pull out one piece of paper from each bag and interpret them using the method and meanings on the following pages. This is great if you're a Witch on a budget, and they could also be a discreet form of divination if you are practicing your Craft in the broom closet.

To use:

Draw a circle of about 8 inches in diameter. Hold the dice in your hands and spend a moment thinking about the situation you want guidance with. Clearly focus your thoughts and intentions and then roll the dice when your intuition tells you to.

Some readers roll the dice again if any fall out of the circle, others give special meanings to the dice that fall outside the circle, and some only read the dice that fall in the circle. Do what feels right to you. If you want to include the dice that fall out of the circle too, their meanings are:

☾ **ONE DICE FALLING OUTSIDE THE CIRCLE**—Difficulties or upset.
☾ **TWO DICE FALLING OUTSIDE THE CIRCLE**—Arguments or disagreements.
☾ **THREE DICE FALLING OUTSIDE THE CIRCLE**—Luck or a wish to come true.
☾ **ANY DICE THAT FALL ON THE FLOOR**—Problems, worry or annoyance.

When you are reading a modern set of three divination dice, it is helpful to read the planets as the situation, the zodiac signs as the emotions involved, and the astrological house numbers (the numbered dice) as the part of your life being affected.

PLANETS—
the Situation

((**THE SUN**—The ego, your most basic self, consciousness, vitality, creation.

((**THE MOON**—Emotions, instincts, habits, moods, subconscious.

((**MERCURY**—The mind, communication, intelligence, reason.

((**VENUS**—Love, attraction, relationships, art, beauty, harmony.

((**MARS**—Aggression, sex, action, desire, courage, passion, competition.

((**JUPITER**—Growth, hope, expansion, luck, abundance, understanding.

((**SATURN**—Discipline, responsibility, ambition, obligation, law.

((**URANUS**—Inspiration, change, eccentricity, chaos, rebellion, reformation.

((**NEPTUNE**—Mysticism, dreams, intuition, psychic abilities, imagination, delusions.

((**PLUTO**—Transformation, power, death, rebirth, evolution.

((**THE NORTH NODE OF THE MOON**—Lessons to be learned, fear of the unknown, fate, the path forward.

((**THE SOUTH NODE OF THE MOON**—The past, karmic baggage, the path you have followed until now.

DIVINATION DICE
ZODIAC SIGNS—
the Emotions

☾ **ARIES**—Impulsivity, competition, letting go, intense reactions to situations.

☾ **TAURUS**—Sensitivity, hurt feelings, emotional responses, holding grudges.

☾ **GEMINI**—Duality, mischievousness, emotions over rationality, cleverness, curiosity.

☾ **CANCER**—Deep emotions, lost friendships, loyalty, nurturing.

☾ **LEO**—Confidence, stamina, leadership, pride, being the center of attention.

☾ **VIRGO**—Rationality, solitude, pickiness, overly critical, striving for more than you can handle.

☾ **LIBRA**—Balance, harmony, or the need to find harmony in a situation that is out of control.

☾ **SCORPIO**—Transformation, truth, honesty, hidden emotions, a need for power.

☾ **SAGITTARIUS**—Adventure, seeking truth, positivity, optimism, a need for relaxation.

☾ **CAPRICORN**— Controlling, possessiveness, business matters, barriers between people.

☾ **AQUARIUS**—Anxiety, unpredictable future, a need for communication, introspection.

☾ **PISCES**—Compassion, escapism, innocence, a person in your life may be acting dishonestly.

ASTROLOGICAL HOUSES–
The Part of You Affected

☾ **1ST**—Personal life, first impressions, identity, physical appearance, consciousness, will.

☾ **2ND**—Finances, wealth, material possessions, desires.

☾ **3RD**—Communication, gossip and rumours, local travel, school, siblings or people tied to you by blood and location.

☾ **4TH**—Home, domestic issues, family, parents or people that act as parental figures.

☾ **5TH**—Fertility, women, children, pregnancy, fun, hobbies.

☾ **6TH**—Health, work, hygiene, daily routines, habits, pets.

☾ **7TH**—Personal partnerships, relationships, marriage.

☾ **8TH**—Sex, occult, death, transformation, loss, inheritance, mortgages, loans, legacies,.

☾ **9TH**—Long-distance travel, religion, spirituality, wisdom, dreams, law, philosophy, divination.

☾ **10TH**—Career, reputation, success, fortune.

☾ **11TH**—Good fortune, friends, friendships, group activities/relationships.

☾ **12TH**—The unconscious, secrets, hidden things, our deepest thoughts, fear, solitude.

CARING FOR
Divination Tools

Divination tools are energetic extensions of you. They enable you to access hidden knowledge and messages from your higher conscious and spirit. As tools that work with energy, they need to be well cared for both physically and energetically to keep them working at their very best. Whether it is tarot, a pendulum, oracle cards, or a crystal ball, your tools will need regular maintenance to keep their energies clear. Treating them with respect is a huge part of this maintenance. When not in use, keep your divination tools covered or wrapped and put them somewhere safe to physically and energetically protect them.

As you would cleanse a crystal before use, the same applies to divination tools—these same methods can be used in this context too (see page 100). Divination tools are conductors of energy and any negativity surrounding them must be cleansed so the energy can flow during a reading. It's a good practice to cleanse them before a reading and when you use your divination tools for the first time after they've been purchased or gifted.

Herbs can be used to cleanse any tool, and not just by smoke cleansing. Simply place your tools on a bed of rosemary or salt for a minimum of four hours to cleanse them of any negative energy. If you wish to cleanse something made of crystal, make sure it's salt safe first. If you're in a pinch, a traditional way to cleanse a tarot or oracle deck is to knock hard on the stack of cards three times, although this is not a deep cleanse, so I only used this method if I don't have time to cleanse them in any another way. Washing tools such as pendulums, crystal balls, and divination dice with mugwort-infused water is a great way to cleanse them and to help enhance your natural psychic and intuitive abilities. If your pendulum is made from crystal, make sure it's water safe beforehand.

Getting to know your tools is also important. This will come through time and use, so make space to connect with them regularly. As long as you are respectful, there is no right or wrong way to do this, so do what you feel is right for you. You could draw a tarot or oracle card each day to get to know your deck. Some Witches sleep with their divination tools under their pillows, to help form a connection with them. Meditation while holding your divination tool is another possible way of connecting with them, but all this is optional. Find the way that works for you.

CARING FOR DIVINATION TOOLS

Look after your tools by cleansing them well before use.

There are many methods and it's completely your choice as to which method feels right.

One way is to put mugwort-infused water in a spray bottle and spray your water safe tools.

Treat your tools with respect, keep them safe when not in use.

Consider keeping them covered in a wrap or cloth and out of the reach of children and pets.

Make time to get to know your cards. Use them regularly or sleep with them under your pillow.

7

EMPATH
CARE

I would describe being an empath as a blessing and a curse. I've been an empath for as long as I can remember, but I didn't realize how many other Witches were empaths too. It's something that affects our personal energy, which can have an impact on our Craft.

An empath is a highly intuitive person who is attuned to the feelings of other people. They take on these emotions as strongly as if they were their own. Empaths have the ability to see and feel things completely from another person's perspective, even if they have no experience of these feelings or viewpoints. It allows empaths to fully understand where another person is coming from, but on another level they will absorb other people's emotional energy, feeling their pain as well as their happiness. Seeing the world from this position can be incredibly draining, and can cause anxiety and unstable moods.

In this chapter, I'll cover the characteristics and traits of an empath to help you decide whether you are an empath. Protecting your energy is vital as an empath for your mental health, so this chapter will talk about different ways you can protect your own energy as an empath and which crystals and herbs can help to support you. You'll also find a collection of useful rituals and meditations, which aims to help you look after yourself and your personal energy while making the most of your gifts.

AM I AN EMPATH?

You absorb the
energy of others.

You have
strong intuition.

AM I AN Empath?

Being an empath means seeing and feeling the world differently to others. There is no one test you can take that will definitively tell you if you are an empath. Having said that, there are several key signs that are very good indicators of empathy. The more of these traits you identify with, the greater the chance that you are an empath yourself.

YOU TAKE ON THE EMOTIONS OF OTHERS

This is the most important trait of an empath. Empaths absorb the energy of those around them, both good and bad. Empaths feel the emotions of others so deeply that sometimes, they can feel physical pain in their bodies as well as mental distress, too. All this takes its toll and can mean empaths often struggle with physical illness or chronic fatigue if they don't protect their own energies or set healthy boundaries for themselves.

The mental toll can mean empaths often experience anxiety and depression in response to the energy they take on from others. Mood swings can be common, particularly when an empath is with a group of people—one minute they can feel sad, then the next they can be happy as they experience the highs and the lows of the energy around them. It can be very uncomfortable, which is why empathy is often described as a curse as well as a gift. This can sometimes make intimate relationships challenging (particularly if the empath lives with their partner, because they can pick up every emotion and mood change). Empaths then have to learn to somehow merge their energy with their partner's, which is hugely difficult and can often feel like an intrusion on personal space.

YOU HAVE STRONG INTUITION

Empaths usually have a strong sense of intuition. They can tell when something feels "off" in a room or with an individual and they are good at knowing when someone is lying or being dishonest. Empaths notice when there is an energetic change in a room and can sense changes to the moods of those around them, even if it's just a subtle change that can't be felt by others. Their sense of knowing goes well beyond conscious reasoning. Empaths know without having any evidence or proof to back up how they feel, but crucially, their knowing is usually accurate.

YOU'RE EASILY OVERWHELMED AND DRAINED

Empaths don't generally like large crowds and can feel easily overwhelmed—they are affected by the emotions and energies of all the people around them, which they feel all at once. This can be incredibly draining. The same can be said when spending time with other people in general. Many empaths prefer one-on-one interactions because it's easier for them to deal with the level of emotions they absorb. Many empaths are unfairly labelled as being "too sensitive" or "emotional" by other people for this reason. This is because the emotions felt by an empath are often constantly heightened. This can lead to feelings of anxiety and stress, particularly if they don't protect their energy and shield themselves from the overwhelming emotions.

YOU'RE A GOOD LISTENER

People come to you with their problems because you are a very good listener. Empaths have the ability to understand where someone is coming from even if they have no personal experience of it themselves. They can intuitively sense what someone is trying to express and because empaths are able to connect with people on a deeper level, they attract those who need a listening ear or a shoulder to cry on. Empaths can guide a conversation in such a way that they make the person feel heard as well as understood.

YOU NEED PERIODS OF SOLITUDE AND PEACE

Personal space and solitude are very important to empaths. Being around people is draining, so empaths need a space to go, alone, where they are not bombarded by others emotions. It is almost like a time of detox from all the energy they have picked up. Empaths can also be extra sensitive to sudden or loud noise. This makes them more likely to withdraw from social situations or even try to avoid them completely. Many empaths prefer to spend time alone, often in a sanctuary they've created as a safe space. My sanctuary is my bedroom and I go there to be alone when I'm overwhelmed. Having a safe place to go is incredibly important to an empath.

YOU LOVE NATURE AND ANIMALS

Nature and animals recharge the batteries of empaths. So much of life is draining, but the life flowing through the natural world replenishes and restores. Spending time on a nature walk can be a form of cleansing, as Mother Nature works to rebalance your personal energy. Empaths are also particularly good with animals. Animals do not bombard us with complex or negative energies, so for an empath, spending time with them is relaxing, soothing, and is a welcome time out.

AM I AN EMPATH?

You're a good listener.

You need periods of
solitude and peace.

You love nature
and animals.

PROTECTION & SELF-CARE
for Empaths

Empaths absorb many different energies as they go about their daily lives, and this can have an impact on their physical, mental, and emotional health. If you are an empath, it's crucial that you learn how to protect your own personal energy, so that the energies of others do not have a negative impact on your well-being. Empathy is a gift, but this gift must be managed properly so you can balance and control the amount of emotion you take on.

There are many ways to protect your energy, from the use of crystals and herbs (I talk about these in detail on pages 141 and 143), to visualization, meditation, and rituals. This section will contain a mixture of all these methods to help you protect your energy. Regardless of what methods you choose to use, they are vital acts of self-care. Seeing them as acts of self-care is important because they are ways that can help you manage your gift. Self-care is not selfish; it is a necessary move to look after your well-being by protecting your own energy.

SHIELDING EXERCISES FOR EMPATHS

The most important (and common) type of protection is shielding, which is where you create an energetic force field around yourself to deflect unwanted energies or emotions. Here are two shielding techniques I use regularly which will help you to protect your own energy anytime and anywhere, like when you're in a crowded place.

Mirror exercise

1. Breathe in and, wherever you are, visualize that you have mirrors all around you, to the sides, above, and below.
2. Visualize that the reflective sides of the mirrors are facing outward, away from you. The mirrors will reflect and shield you from any emotion and energy that comes your way. Keep the mirrors around you for as long as you need shielding.
3. If you feel you need extra protection, visualize another row of mirrors standing around you, reflecting outward, making your shield twice as powerful and effective.

Glowing light exercise

1. Visualize a white light glowing from the Solar Plexus (the Third Chakra, our energy center, which is located between your belly button and sternum).
2. See it expand slowly and fill up every part of your body, from head to toe, with a warming white protective haze.
3. Visualize it shining beyond your physical body to create a shield all around you.

PROTECTION AND SELF-CARE FOR EMPATHS

Protection is crucial for empaths because they absorb the energy of other people and become easily overwhelmed by the emotion this causes. These are just some of the important ways empaths can protect their energy.

Practice shielding
visualizations.

Practice grounding
visualizations.

Make a grounding,
protective talisman.

Practice and meditate
on detachment.

GROUNDING EXERCISES
for Empaths

Being grounded helps to balance your personal energy, which is crucial if you are constantly being bombarded by the destabilizing energies of your surroundings. This visualization helps remove any excess or unwanted energy trapped in your body.

Grounding visualization

1. Sit somewhere comfortable with your feet on the ground, breathing steadily.
2. Visualize a white light entering the top of your head and slowly flowing downward.
3. When you feel the white light reaching a place where you are holding onto the energies and emotions of others, acknowledge them, before visualizing the white light engulfing and pushing them downward toward the ground.

4. As the white light flows toward your feet, imagine it pushing all the unwanted energy out of your body and into the ground, like a cleanse.

Take your time with this visualization, removing every bit of unwanted energy. This exercise is also good for removing stagnant energy when you need an energy boost.

Make a grounding talisman

Some Witches use a talisman to help them reground and balance their energies. A talisman can be a piece of jewelry that is filled with magickal protective powers, or anything you feel drawn to. It can bring protection and remove any unwanted energies attached to you, so you maintain balance of your own energies.

1. Cleanse the item you've chosen.
2. Hold the item in your hand and infuse it with grounding energy. Think about the places where you have felt most grounded. Is it at home? In your mother's kitchen, or outside on a nature walk? To charge this item, mentally revisit these times where you felt grounded and safe. Do this for as long as you feel is right. To add to the power of your talisman, do this visualization in one of the places that you felt most grounded.
3. You could also bury your talisman for 24 hours in the ground (if it won't be damaged), or in a plant pot full of soil, to fill it with grounding and stabilizing energy.
4. Get to know your talisman. Wear or carry it throughout the day and in stressful situations, or when you have been emotionally triggered, and notice how it supports and grounds you. You can even use it as a focus for meditation.

I RELEASE THE DESIRE
FOR CONTROL

DETACHMENT EXERCISE
for Empaths

Empaths are very good at taking on the energy of others. This can be very overwhelming and it's important that you know how to stop this when it gets too much. Detachment is a very useful way to control what energies you absorb. As with all these methods of protection and self-care, they take time and practice to master, so don't be discouraged if at first you find these techniques difficult. Keep going!

There are several ways to practice loving detachment and build it into your life. They're not about completely cutting you off from the world around you but rather creating a healthy space between you and the energies of others, so they don't have a negative impact on your well-being.

Loving detachment exercise

☾ Sit and meditate on the things you have strong emotional responses to and the reasons why. To become detached, it's crucial that you understand and have greater awareness for the reasons why you react as you do.

☾ Meditate on the difference between reacting and responding—try not to react but instead respond to a stressful situation. Reacting is automatic, whereas a response is about taking a breath and giving a thought-out reply.

☾ Reflect on your need to fix everyone's problems and the pressure that brings. Why do you feel like this? Could it be that you desire to help others is a subconscious desire to help yourself?

☾ Meditate on control—remember that you can't control others, regardless of how much your try. Being detached is about releasing the desire for control so you can focus on your own growth. You can still be there for others, but at a healthy emotional distance.

HERBS FOR EMPATHS

3. 4.

2. 5.

1. 6.

1. Chamomile—Aids relaxation, eases anxiety and insomnia
2. Cloves—Protects, dispels negative energy
3. Dandelion—Releases anger, detoxifies, protects
4. Ginseng—Improves emotional balance
5. Hawthorn berries—Heals, helps to stop you absorbing the emotions of others
6. Lavender—Relaxes nerves, gently protects, eases anxiety

HERBS
for empaths

Empaths can make use of a wide range of herbs and spices for emotional and energetic protection and there are many ways to incorporate them into your practice. This is just a selection of the most beneficial but easily available herbs for empaths, but I encourage you to do more research to find others. I have also included recipes and spells from my grimoire, but feel free to rework or tweak them so they work better for you!

SPELL BAGS

One of the easiest ways to protect yourself is to make a spell bag with herbs of your choice in, and carry it around with you throughout the day to benefit from their magickal properties. One of my favorite combinations in a spell bag is cloves, skullcap, and lavender to bring protection and help regulate emotions.

SPELL JARS

Using a mixture of herbs along with corresponding crystals (see Chapter 5) in a spell jar is a good way to blend and concentrate their magickal energies. Choose a small bottle so you're able to carry it in your bag or pocket. An empathic protective spell jar I have found to be very effective includes salt, cloves, black pepper, dandelion flowers, and black obsidian. Seal the jar by dripping black wax around the lid.

OILS

These can be used in a variety of ways for protection. You can anoint yourself with a protection oil on your pulse points or anoint a black candle with oil then roll it in herbs such as basil, thyme, and dill for a simple protection spell. Make a protection oil using equal parts of basil, dandelion, raspberry leaves, vervain, and lavender in an oil such as sunflower or grapeseed oil. Leave it to infuse for a month before use.

INCENSE

Herbs can be burned as incense to bring protection and rid your home or space of any unwanted energy. For a cleansing and protective blend use equal parts of lavender, common garden sage, dandelion root, pine needles, and rosemary, and burn on a hot charcoal disc.

CLEANSING BATH SOAKS

One of the traits of an empath is to absorb the emotions of others but herbs can be used to cleanse you of this unwanted energy. This is crucial to rebalancing your personal energy. You can do this by making an empath detox bath of 1 part salt and 3 parts chamomile flowers, rosemary, and lavender (or two drops of lavender essential oil). ***Caution:*** *If you have sensitive or allergic reaction prone skin, always perform a patch test first (see page 40).*

BLUE SANDSTONE
Deflects negativity,
eases anxiety,
and promotes
emotional stability.

SMOKY QUARTZ
Cleanses its
environment
and encourages
positive energy.

HEMATITE
Creates a protective
shield from
negative energies.

CRYSTALS
FOR
EMPATHS

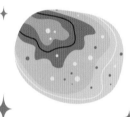

ROSE QUARTZ
Promotes inner peace
and harmony,
and heals emotionally.

LEPIDOLITE
Balances, calms, and
heals emotionally.

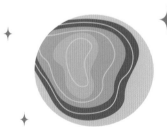

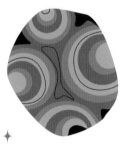

MOONSTONE
Stabilizes emotions
and encourages
personal growth.

MALACHITE
Clears stagnant and
negative energies.

CRYSTALS
for Empaths

Just as meditation, visualization, and herbs can be used by empaths to help protect, ground, and rebalance personal energy, crystals are also another way empaths can protect their energy. The good thing about working with crystals is that they are so versatile and can be incorporated into your practice in so many ways. Here's a collection of the most helpful crystals, along with different ways you can use them in your practice.

JEWELRY

One of the easiest ways to work with crystals as an empath is to wear them as jewelry. Wearing your chosen crystals as a bracelet, pendant, or ring is a great way to keep crystals with you to fully benefit from their magickal properties. I can't go anywhere without my blue sandstone and amethyst bracelet!

CARRY IN YOUR POCKET

Crystals, usually tumbled, can also be carried in your pocket rather than wearing them as jewelry. As an empath it's even more important to cleanse these crystals frequently to remove all the negative energy they have picked up while protecting and shielding you. I like to cleanse the crystal bracelets I wear by placing them in a selenite bowl when I take them off each night, but find a routine that feels right to you.

SPELL BAG

Using crystals in a spell bag is another way you can benefit from their magickal properties on the move. Place your chosen crystals and place in a colored bag that aligns with your intention. As empaths, we absorb the emotions of others, which can have a negative impact on our own emotions. For a bag to help emotional stability, I place moonstone, lepidolite, amazonite, and clear quartz in a brown bag and carry it with me in my pocket for grounding and protection.

ELIXIRS

Making an elixir allows you to ingest the magickal energy of the crystals you use (see pages 102 and 109 for information on how to make elixirs, and crystals that are safe to make elixirs from). I like to make a blend of smoky and rose quartz to cleanse me of any unwanted energy while promoting inner peace and positivity.

USE AT HOME

Crystals can also be used in the home to give energetic protection for empaths. Smoky quartz and malachite are great crystals to use for this purpose, as they cleanse the environment they're placed in of any negative and stagnant energy. Use them alongside clear quartz which will help to amplify these properties of the crystals it is placed with.

SHADOW WORK IS THE PATH OF THE WARRIOR

8
SHADOW WORK

While light should always have a place within Witchcraft and in our own personal spiritual journeys, so, too, should shadow and darkness. Sometimes it's easier to focus on the light, so we push the dark away, until something happens that forces us to confront it again. A balance must be struck between light and dark, so there isn't more of one than the other. This is difficult, but it's essential that we embrace the dark as well as the light rather than ignore or avoid it.

This can sound scary, but by embracing your own shadow, you can learn to understand yourself better. It can lay the foundations that will enable you to live your life more authentically.

Every person has a shadow self, which is no bad thing. This part of your being is filled with the things you might be hiding, repressing, or ignoring, as well as things you are ashamed or frightened of. If we don't try to understand our shadows, we will never fully understand ourselves and why we do the things we do. It helps us to embrace all that we are, not just the good bits, which is a radical act of self-love, care, and acceptance.

Let's start your shadow journey!

SHADOW WORK
CAN TRANSFORM
YOU

HOW TO BEGIN
Shadow Work

Shadow work is about exploring the darker depths of our souls to confront the things that lay in the shadows. It's not an easy journey to take, but the thing is, it isn't meant to be easy. Shadow work asks us to confront emotions such as pain, grief, and trauma, which is not easy, but is worth it.

The things that push us out of our comfort zones take us mentally to the places where personal growth and healing can occur because you can then align more fully with your true self. This might sound daunting, but I will help you get started. You might even find that you already practice shadow work in your own life without realizing it.

HELPING YOUR CRAFT

Shadow work is all about introspection and being present in everyday life, something that is associated with practices such as meditation and yoga. It can facilitate deep healing and can help you achieve good mental health and a sense of well-being. Although this is not the kind of Witchcraft that involves magick, anything that can help your grow and become more aware of yourself and who you are will have a positive and empowering impact on your Craft. It will raise the vibrations of your energy, which, in turn, have an impact on the spells you cast and the rituals you perform.

It can be very difficult to know where to begin. The thought of starting shadow work can be intimidating enough, let alone trying to figure out how to do it.

ONE THING AT A TIME

Whatever your approach, it's a good practice to focus on only one thing at a time. Try to resist the temptation to work through many different areas of your life at the same time. Trying to simultaneously bring into the light everything that hides within your shadow self would be completely overwhelming. It's important to look after yourself as you do shadow work, so you are not hit by so many different emotions. Although shadow work is often difficult, it's worth every minute of your time because of the transformative effect it can have on your mental health and well-being.

HOW TO BEGIN
Shadow Work

OBSERVE YOUR FEELINGS AND REACTIONS

A good place to start your shadow work journey is to look at the things that trigger you emotionally—they can guide you to areas of your subconscious where healing is needed. The idea is to observe how you feel and react to everyday situations but to do so without judgement, being as far removed in an emotional sense as possible. If you try to observe your response to triggers when you are immersed deeply in your emotions, the emotions will take over and you will not be able to objectively examine why you react in the way that you do. It's a process of self-awareness, and it can be hard, but I encourage you to keep going.

It is difficult to try and be objective when it comes to our emotions, but it's an ability you can develop if you commit time and patience to self-observation. By stepping back and viewing your responses, judgements, and behavior from a place of objectivity, you can look honestly within yourself to critically analyze the trigger and address the root causes. You can also see any behavioral patterns emerging that will point to other areas that need your attention. This isn't easy, nor is it an opportunity to unfairly beat yourself up over the things you might have done

wrong, but rather it's a chance to understand why you act the way you do and bring healing and awareness to the areas that need it most.

PRACTICE EMOTIONAL ENQUIRY

Emotional enquiry is a practice that goes hand in hand with observing your feelings. When it comes to analyzing your emotions and behavior after a period of stress, take a step back so that you can emotionally detach yourself enough to ask constructive questions that are not emotionally influenced. Constructive questions could be:

"Why do I feel the way I do?"
"Why does it trigger me?"
"Is there something in my past that causes me to feel like this now?"

These questions try to get to the heart of your shadow self. Asking yourself direct questions like this will give you more information and a better understanding of the situation, but only if you answer honestly. That's the key to all shadow work—being truly honest with yourself. It's only through your truth and emotion that you can connect and get to know what lies in your shadow.

HOW TO BEGIN SHADOW WORK

Observe your reactions to different issues and situations, and look for behavioral patterns.

Don't overload yourself. Regardless of the method you choose, pick one thing to focus on at a time.

Practice emotional enquiry—ask yourself why you're feeling as you do when you're triggered. Question why you react as you do.

HOW TO BEGIN
Shadow Work

PROJECTION

Projection is the next phase of emotional enquiry because it involves asking yourself probing questions that can uncover emotions hiding beneath the surface. This is the process of examining whether or not we project our deepest emotions onto others. It confronts those things we may have repressed.

When something stressful or triggering happens, allow yourself to step back and ask: "Am I projecting anything onto this situation—if so, why?" Often you may be placing your unconscious issues onto a current situation, which then becomes triggering. To stop and ask yourself this question brings reality into the situation, but it also brings what is unconscious into the light. What you are projecting shines a light on areas that need further examination and understanding.

This can be a very effective technique to do at any time. Even when the situation isn't stressful, we can all be guilty of projection to some degree. This shadow work technique isn't easy and will take practice, but bear with it because it's a powerful tool to understand your shadow self better. See the people around you as mirrors, reflecting back the parts of your unconscious self that needs healing.

PRACTICE BEING PRESENT

This is one of the most important elements of shadow work. We all possess the ability to be mindful, although it takes practice to be able to make the very most of it. Mindfulness is not necessarily meant to be relaxing. When you allow yourself to live in the moment and be present every day, you can start to connect with the parts of yourself that have remained hidden—your shadow. Healing can begin when you confront how you feel in the here and now.

This can be done in many ways, but it all involves setting aside regular time for your mindfulness practice. This could be as little as 5 minutes a day where you make a conscious effort to focus on the present moment and just "be." If your mind wanders, don't be hard on yourself. Pay attention to where your thoughts go, the emotions you feel, and the pictures that form in your mind but then guide your mind back to the present. Don't make a judgement about the things you think and see—just let them pass for the time you are practicing mindfulness. See page 167 for a meditation practice.

Afterward, reflect on the feelings your meditation raised because they can be used to unlock aspects of your own shadow. For example, feelings of guilt can indicate you're living your life based on the expectations of others rather than doing what you feel is right for you.

HOW TO BEGIN SHADOW WORK

During times of stress, ask yourself if you are projecting your own subconscious fears and desires.

Meditate on the aspects of your shadow to get to know it better. Journal prompts can also be used for meditation.

Practice being present and conscious in everyday life rather than living too much in the past or the future.

SHADOW WORK:
Journaling & Prompts

Another practical way to do shadow work is through journaling. This is probably my favorite method and is another great place to start your shadow journey. Writing down your innermost thoughts and feelings can be an amazing tool to help increase your self-awareness and guide you through the process of shadow work. You can write freely, or you can use journal prompts to help give your shadow work structure, allowing you to control the intensity. You can use more gentle prompts to start with, working your way up to heavier prompts when you feel ready. It's a way to access your subconscious, where you've buried so many emotions, so your first reaction to a journal prompt is often the most honest answer. Be truthful to yourself. Although this is a difficult process, understanding yourself more can also help you to uncover repressed gifts and skills you never knew you had!

Here is a collection of different journal prompts I have used and found helpful to get you started. Feel free to use them as they are or modify them to suit your needs. Taking one prompt at a time will help the process feel less overwhelming.

Prompts

1. How would you describe yourself?
2. How would other people describe you? How do you feel about that?
3. What are your best and worst character traits?
4. What do you like and dislike about yourself?
5. What part of you doesn't feel heard?
6. What would you like to say?
7. What makes you happy?
8. Who do you trust the most? Why?
9. Do you have issues with trust?
10. What things triggers you the most? Why are these things a trigger for you?
11. What things are you judgemental about?
12. How do you pass judgement on yourself?
13. When is the last time you felt let down? Why?
14. Who has the most influence over you in your life? Is it a healthy influence?
15. How often do you lie to yourself or others?
16. Is any part of you in denial?
17. What is your biggest fear? Why?
18. What irrational fear do you have? Why?
19. What grudges do you hold? Why? Are they rational?
20. Do you hold on to any resentment? Towards whom? Why?

SHADOW WORK:
JOURNALING AND PROMPTS

Many people find journaling a great tool for shadow work and it is a great place to start your shadow journey.

You can control the intensity of the questions. Although shadow work is hard, it should not emotionally overwhelm you.

Using journal prompts is a practical way to structure your shadow work.

When using these prompts, it's important you answer the questions honestly. Often your first response is the honest one.

Using prompts for shadow work is not easy, but it can also uncover gifts you have repressed for years and didn't know you had.

SHADOW WORK:
Tarot & Oracle Spreads

Cartomancy, or the use of tarot and oracle cards, can be a very useful tool for shadow work. Using cartomancy in specifically designed shadow work spreads can be particularly helpful if you are struggling to know where to start—it offers structured guidance that can give you a solid place to begin. It can help to connect you with your subconscious and draw out those things from your shadows that help us to understand ourselves better.

Using tarot and oracle spreads in this way goes hand in hand with journaling because the cards you have pulled can give you a starting point to explore the themes they raise. But tarot and oracle cards don't have to be part of an elaborate spread to give insight. When you hit a blockage, you can ask a simple question such as: "What issue is causing this blockage?" and then pull a card. You can use the information the card gives to try and delve under the surface of the obstacle, to try and understand what really lies behind it. You could also do the same when you find that you're triggered by something, by asking questions such as: "Why am I triggered by this?"; or "What is causing this trigger?" before pulling a card and exploring the answer through journaling.

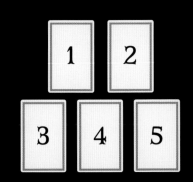

A spread for understanding fear

1. What do I fear right now?
2. Why do I fear this?
3. How does this fear manifest in my life?
4. What is the root of this fear?
5. How can I confront this fear?

A spread for overcoming obstacles

1. What is preventing me from moving forward?
2. Why is it blocking my path?
3. What deeper issues does it raise?
4. How do I deal with these issues?
5. What aspects of my shadow self do I need to confront to move forward?

A spread for exploring your shadow self

1. What shadow aspect do I need to focus on now?
2. What do I need to focus on this aspect?
3. What needs to be released to facilitate healing?
4. How can I do this in the best way?
5. What hard truths must I acknowledge to help me heal?
6. What lesson can examining this shadow aspect teach?
7. How can I use this lesson and information to help me in my life right now?

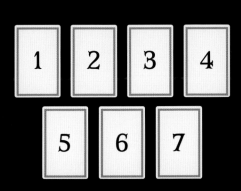

HERBS AND CRYSTALS
FOR SHADOW WORK

EUCALYPTUS
Brings clarity and calm.

BLACK MOONSTONE
An empowering stone that
supports change and
transformation.

COMMON GARDEN SAGE
Reduces stress
and calms.

LAPIS LAZULI
Helps you to understand
your shadow self, to
heal, and to reclaim
your power.

PASSION FLOWER
Brings deep
peace and calm in
stressful situations.

BLACK ONYX
Helps to find grounding,
stability, and calm when
you feel emotionally
overwhelmed.

BURDOCK ROOT
A deep healer that
wards off negativity.

JET
Helps release
repressed emotions.

CYPRESS
Taps into inner wisdom,
and helps you move on
from things that don't
serve you.

SHADOW WORK:
Crystals & Herbs

Shadow work is certainly not easy. You are journeying deep within you, and stirring up a lot of raw emotion. Using certain crystals and herbs can help to support you through the process.

CRYSTALS

These can be carried in your pocket or bag (I carry mine in my bra!), used in crystal grids and placed nearby, or held when you do your shadow work such as journaling, meditation, and tarot readings. Crystals such as black moonstone support inner change and can be empowering through your journey. It is a good stone to have with you when you are exploring your shadow self because it empowers and enhances mental agility to help you to work though the emotions that arise.

Being grounded is important during this process, so crystals such as black onyx, black tourmaline, and hematite are good to carry with you in a pouch or your pocket to help balance your energy. Jet is a stone of protection and purification and will help you release repressed emotions. Be aware, jet can release many repressed emotions all at once, almost like opening a floodgate. Just take your time to work through each emotion that it helps to raise. Jet is a good crystal to use during shadow work but I wouldn't recommend you carry it with you. To help heal the wounds that shadow work exposes, crystals such as lapis lazuli, selenite, and rose quartz can bring a healing energy that helps you understand your shadow self better.

HERBS

Herbs can be used to support your shadow work in many ways. They can be burned as incense, made into tinctures, carried in spell bags, used as essential oils, and some can be drunk as tea. A combination of lavender, rosemary, chamomile, myrrh, and passionflower burned as incense can really help to create a calm atmosphere when doing shadow work such as journaling and meditation. Lavender can also be burned as an essential oil for the same purpose. Eucalyptus and cypress are also great to use as essential oils— eucalyptus can be placed on your pulse points to help you find clarity and strength while you continue your shadow journey, and you can anoint your forehead with cypress essential oil to help you move on from the things that no longer serve you. Burdock root can be dried and then made into a tea. It is a deep healer and, coupled with chamomile and lemon balm, makes the perfect tea to drink during a shadow work. With tea and incense, you can use herbs to create an atmosphere that will support you as well as help you explore inward.

SHADOW WORK:
SELF-CARE

Self-care is an essential part of preparing yourself for shadow work.

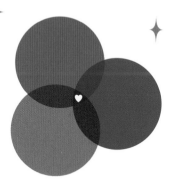

It is about looking after your emotional, physical, and mental well-being.

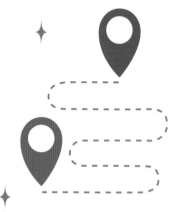

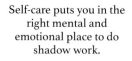

Self-care puts you in the right mental and emotional place to do shadow work.

Self-care comes in many forms so it's important you find the things that help you and your journey.

Meditation, visualization, spells, and ritual baths are just some of the many ways you can practice self-care.

SHADOW WORK:
Self-Care

When doing shadow work, it's essential that you look after yourself properly. Self-care is vital—it supports the whole process of your inner journey. Shadow work can be tough enough, but without preparing yourself first, the journey will be much harder. Self-care, on a deeper level, is about looking after your mind and emotions so you are in the right place to do shadow work. Self-love is also important too; it gives a solid foundation on which the inner work can build.

Self-love meditation

1. Sit somewhere comfy and, if you have some available, hold a piece of rose quartz in your hand throughout the ritual. Don't worry if you don't have any available to you, you can still do the meditation without it.

2. Ground and center your energy by bringing your attention to the heart chakra, which sits in the middle of your chest. The heart chakra is the center of love and healing in the body and, by activating this, you can help to grow feelings of love within yourself. It is the basis for this self-love ritual.

3. When you are ready, bring focus to your breathing. Every time you breathe in, visualize yourself taking in the energy from your surroundings and, when you exhale, your heart chakra begins to grow. Visualize it as a bright white light and every time you exhale, this light gets brighter and brighter as your heart chakra is strengthened. Keep doing this, at a natural rhythm of breathing for you, until you are filled with light. Once you are full, visualize this light spilling out slowly into the space you're sat in with every exhale, until the whole room is filled with it. If at any point you feel resistance to this growing love, direct this energy toward your heart chakra, where it will be dissolved and transformed into light.

4. Once the room is filled, slowly inhale and exhale and say out loud "I am worthy, I am capable, I am strong, I am confident, I am loved." Don't just say the words, feel them too. As you speak, feel the love in the room surround and support you as you breath love into your words. Repeat these affirmations over and over. Do this for as long as you feel you need to feel strengthened by this loving energy. If you have used a piece of rose quartz in your ritual, keep it with you as a talisman.

EMOTIONAL RELEASE
& Healing Rituals

When shadow work gets too much and you are feeling overwhelmed, these simple rituals can help you rebalance your energy.

Emotional release ritual

You will need:

- ☾ 1 green or white candle (for emotional healing)
- ☾ 1 black or white candle (for release)
- ☾ Crystals: 1 piece of jet (for release) and rose quartz (to soften the emotional release and to replace any unwanted energy with love)
- ☾ Paper and pen
- ☾ A heatproof dish
- ☾ Dried rosemary and rose petals

1. Cleanse your tools and space first.
2. Once you're ready, light the candles and hold the jet and rose quartz in your hand, and sit for a moment. Think about the emotions you are feeling now—what do you want to release? It could be your emotions about a situation, person, or event or it could be just certain feelings such as anger or anxiety. Set the crystals aside and whatever you want to release, write it all down on a piece of paper, going into as much detail as possible so your intent is focused. While you're doing this, allow yourself to cry if you need to—this can be an amazing form of release.
3. When you are ready, in a heatproof dish, burn the paper completely down to ashes as you visualize yourself beginning to release the emotions you have written about. While it's burning, throw in some dried rosemary to aid emotional release, and rose petals to help healing.
4. Collect the ash when it's all burned down and has cooled. Place it in the palm of your hand. Take your time and, when you feel ready (this bit is best done outside), blow all the ash from your hand, into the air, to symbolize complete release.
5. Let the candles burn out to complete the ritual.

EMOTIONAL HEALING RITUAL BATH

You will need:
Lavender, lemon balm, chamomile, and linden (if you have sensitive or allergy prone
skin, you must perform a patch test before any ritual bath)
Rose quartz and amethyst
1 green candle

Place all the ingredients loose into a hot bath or into a small cotton bag and use like a
teabag to prevent clogged drains. Place the rose quartz and amethyst in the water
(they're water safe) or leave next to the green candle, to symbolize emotional healing.

ENERGY =
CHANGE
CHANGE =
GROWTH

9

ENERGY BALANCING TECHNIQUES

The magickal techniques of breathwork, meditation, grounding, and visualization form the foundations of Witchcraft. You might already be familiar with these techniques because they are not skills that necessarily relate to the practice of the Craft alone. If you're not already familiar with these practices, the good thing is it's relatively easy to learn the basics. When understood and practiced well, breathwork, meditation, grounding, and visualization enables us to control our own energies, minds, and bodies, which is crucial for any kind of magick. Magick is fundamentally about using our own energies to manipulate the natural forces around us to bring about change to our environment. Having a greater command over your personal energies will help to improve the success of your spells. It gives you the skills to control and direct this energy to where it's needed.

These techniques are not just for magick but for self-care too. Grounding is a way to stabilize your energy and connect with the earthly energies around you. If practiced well, it can help to bring about a sense of inner balance. Good breathwork is very useful for self-care and can help to achieve a greater sense of calm. Meditation can help you to achieve a deep state of relaxation, and visualization can improve concentration and reduce anxiety.

BREATHWORK

Breath is the energy that flows through our bodies. It's the force of life itself. It might seem strange to have a section on a topic so natural to us as breathing, but most of us don't necessarily breathe correctly. For the majority of us, our breathing tends to be shallow and come from the chest (known as thoracic breathing) rather than the belly, but a good technique would include both thoracic and belly breathing. Correct breathing should ideally come from the belly first, then inflate the chest and then the area around your collarbone—this way, you fill up the whole of your lungs from bottom to top rather than using than just using the upper part.

Controlling our breathing allows us to control part of our physical bodies, and their functions, and puts us in touch with our own energy. This is important in spell casting, but it also can have an impact on your sense of well-being by bringing a sense of calm, reducing anxiety, and helping you center yourself and your energy. It can be helpful in the removal of spiritual blocks within the body and mind, too.

Breathwork is about being able to consciously use your breath to bypass the mind and enter a different state of awareness. If you practice yoga, this might already sound familiar—as Witches, it's a technique that brings many benefits, both mundane and magickal. There are many types of breathwork, but here are two.

4-7-8 breathing

1. Inhale through your nose for 4 seconds.
2. Hold your breath for 7 seconds.
3. Exhale through your mouth for 8 seconds.
4. Repeat this cycle at least 4 times.

Square or 4-4-4-4 breathing

If you're looking for a boost of energy, this is great breathwork to do before a spell or ritual because it will slow down your heart rate. It makes you feel more relaxed but also sharpens your concentration, so you can focus your energy and attention on your magick.

1. Release all the air from your lungs and hold your breath for 4 seconds.
2. Breathe through your nose for 4 seconds
3. Hold your breath for another 4 seconds.
4. Exhale out of your nose for 4 seconds.
5. Repeat this cycle at least 4–5 times.

Focus on this image as you practice your breathing and imagine
your lungs filling with fresh air.

If you can't light a candle, or are out and about and need to ground yourself, focus on the candle in this book, imagining the flames gently flickering.

MEDITATION

Meditation is an ancient wellness practice that is associated with many spiritual traditions. It's a term most of us have heard before and many may already practice it in one form or another. Meditation can be practiced as part of a religious or a spiritual path, or even as secular mindfulness. The great thing is that anyone can meditate, but it does take time to learn. The key word is consistency—to learn, you must set aside some time for practice every day. When you first begin, 5–10 minutes of meditation each day is a good amount of time to aim for. It takes time for you to train your mind to think in this new way, so be patient with yourself and the process, and stick with it.

Don't worry if at first you have trouble controlling your thoughts—contrary to popular belief, meditation is not about completely clearing your mind of all thought but rather giving you the space to acknowledge what you feel and think, and to then train your mind to let these thoughts pass by. Meditation is important to the practice of Witchcraft because it helps us develop a greater sense of awareness of our own personal energy and the energy of the environment around us. Regular meditation can enhance your sense of intuition because your relaxed state allows you to tap into your higher self without being hindered by your day-to-day thoughts.

Setting the scene for meditation is crucial and getting comfortable is important. Some people like to light incense and candles, and others like to play repetitive sounds such as chanting or drumming. Whatever way you choose, do what feels right to you.

A simple way I like to use to induce a meditative state is to light a candle or incense and focus on the flame and smoke as intently as possible. Using the 4-4-4-4 breathwork technique (see page 164) can also help to achieve a relaxed state if repeated for a few minutes or more. Once you are in this state of mind, allow your thoughts to pass you by—don't judge or hold on to them. If you catch yourself thinking, stop your thoughts, then allow them to pass through your mind. Observing the sensations you feel in your body or focusing on an object while you are in a meditative state are good ways to keep your attention and concentration focused.

VISUALIZATION

This is the technique where we use our imagination to generate images in our mind's eye. It's something we all do in one form or another, often without even thinking. In Witchcraft, visualization is used to picture the things we want to manifest in the physical world. It's a natural skill we are all born with, but as we get older, many adults can lose touch with the ability to visualize as well as they once did. The good news is that visualization is a skill we never lose, even if you don't consider yourself to be a very visual person.

Visualization is an important technique for ritual and spell work. As you raise energy, you can use it to direct where you want it to go. It brings the things you're working toward closer into reality and concentrates the energy of your spell, giving your workings a boost. Practicing visualization before and during your spells also helps you to align yourself with the exact intentions you have for your magick, intensifying their effect.

This simple visualization exercise will improve your visualization skills if practiced regularly.

Apple visualization

1. All you need is an apple (but any fruit will do). Hold it in your hands—see how it looks, feels, what color it is, and any other little details you might notice.

2. Put the apple down and close your eyes.

3. Picture it in your mind. How did it feel? What color was it?

4. Once you have the apple in your mind's eye, zoom in closer—what can you see? Are there any little details on the surface you missed before?

5. Zoom in closer still—what do you see? Look at the details in your mind's eye.

6. Next, zoom out to a comfortable distance and then visualize the apple slowly turning so you can see it from the top and bottom. What can you see?

7. Open your eye. Cut the apple in half, then close your eyes again. Visualize the apple in your mind, but this time cut in half. How does the apple look inside? What can you smell? Take your time to observe every detail.

8. Now take a piece of the apple and bite into it. What does it taste like? Is it sweet? Sour? Take your time to savor the flavor.

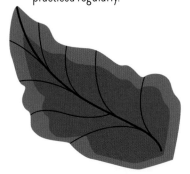

Practice your visualization by focusing on this apple, and carrying
out the steps on the page opposite using pure imagination.

GROUNDING

Grounding, or Earthing, is a form of meditation that helps to keep our mind in the present moment, connecting us to our own physical bodies and to the energies of Mother Earth. It's one of the most important ways a Witch can receive energy from the Earth but also release any excess energy we may be carrying. Grounding is also one of the important magickal self-care tools in a Witch's arsenal. It can be used to restore a sense of balance when we are feeling overwhelmed by our thoughts and emotions and can also help to promote calm, and ease anxiety.

Many Witches (myself included) ground themselves before any ritual or spell work to balance their energy but also to focus their concentration on the present moment and the magick at hand. Grounding is a useful technique to deploy after spell work too, as a means of releasing the excess energy you may have picked up through your magickal workings.

Grounding is a fairly easy technique to learn and there are many ways in which to do it, so choose the method that feels right to you. My favorite way to ground myself is by using a simple tree-grounding exercise that helps to connect me to the energies of the Earth. As this is a visualization exercise, it can be done anywhere, although I find it has the best effects when I practice it somewhere quiet outside.

Tree grounding exercise

1. Sit somewhere quiet, with your feet on the floor. Start breathing in deeply through your nose, and out through your mouth.

2. When you're ready, imagine you are a tree standing strong and proud in the ground.

3. Bring awareness to your feet and how they feel firmly anchored to the ground.

4. Imagine you have roots extending from the bottom of your feet to reach into the Earth.

5. Visualize these roots as they push through the soil, spreading downward, and outward, as they anchor you to the Earth.

6. With each exhale, push any extra or unwanted energies down your body, towards your feet, and out through your roots.

7. As you do this, feel any stress or tension leave your body, starting from your head, then your shoulders, chest, stomach, hips, and then your legs.

8. Keep pushing until you feel all this energy has been released.

9. To replenish lost energy, now visualize your roots absorbing white energy from the soil. Feel the light enter your feet, move up your legs, and slowly fill up your whole body.

10. Allow the energy of the Earth to create a feeling of balance and well-being. Concentrate on this feeling for as long as you need to.

Focus on this mighty tree to help you carry out the visualization
exercise on the page opposite.

Conclusion

Our personal energy is the most important and powerful tool we possess. It's crucial for the practice of Witchcraft and is essential for our sense of well-being. Taking care of our energy also allows us to grow, flourish, and align ourselves with higher realms of consciousness. This can mean protecting your energy as an empath as well as seeking to understand your shadow side through shadow work. It can also mean working with your body, remembering that just as the natural world goes through its own seasons, so do our own personal energies.

I truly hope this book has helped you to connect with your own energy, its rhythms, as well as the different natural and magickal ways you can use to look after it. I also hope this book encourages you to incorporate more Earth magick into your practice and connect with the natural world around you. Earth does not only refer to the ground beneath our feet, but also Mother Nature's bounty including crystals, herbs, trees, flowers, salts, resins, as well as the four elements and seasons too. Your path is your own and it is completely your choice as to how you use them in your Craft—but the best guide you can have is your intuition.

Further Reading

ASTROLOGY:
Skye Alexander, Magickal Astrology
Steven Forrest, The Inner Sky
Judy Hall, The Astrology Bible
Joanna Martine Woolfolk, The Only Astrology Book You'll Ever Need.

CRYSTALS:
Scott Cunningham, Crystal, Gem & Metal Magick
Karen Frazier, Crystals for Beginners

Ember Grant, The Book of Crystal Spells
Judy Hall, The Crystal Bible (1, 2 and 3

DIVINATION:
Scott Cunningham, Divination for Beginners.
Liz Dean, The Divination Handbook
Brigit Esselmont, The Ultimate Guide to Tarot Card Meanings
Robyn Valentine, Magickal Tarot

EMPATH CARE:

Tanya Carroll Richardson, Self-Care for Empaths
Sydney Campos, The Empath Experience
Aletheia Luna & Mateo Sol, Awakened Empath
Judith Orloff, The Empath's Survival Guide
Judith Orloff, Thriving as an Empath.

GREEN WITCHCRAFT:

Arin Murphy-Hiscock, The Green Witch.
Paige Vanderbeck, Green Witchcraft.
Juliet Diaz, Plant Witchery
Scott Cunningham, The Encyclopaedia of Magickal Herbs
Judy Ann Nock, The Modern Witchcraft Guide to Magickal Herbs

NON-WICCAN WITCHCRAFT:

D. E. Luet, A Witch's Book of Shadows
Lindsay Squire, Natural Magick

SHADOW WORK:

Aletheia Luna & Mateo Sol, The Awakening Process
Mathew Micheletti, The Inner Work
Morgue, The Path of Shadow: Self and Universal Completion
Connie Zweig, Meeting the Shadow of Spirituality

TRADITIONAL WITCHCRAFT:

Gemma Gary, Traditional Witchcraft: A Book of Cornish Ways
Gemma Gary, The Black Toad
Edain McCoy, Sabbats: A Witch's Approach to Living the Old Ways
Nigel G. Pearson, Wortcunning: A Folk Magick Herbal
Nigel G. Pearson, Walking the Tides: Seasonal Rhythms and Traditional Core in Natural Craft

WICCAN:

Margot Adler, Drawing Down the Moon
Diane Ahlquist, Moon Spells
Skye Alexander, The Modern Guide to Witchcraft: Your Complete Guide to Witches, Covens and Spells
Deborah Blake, Everyday Witchcraft
Raymond Buckland, Complete Books of Witchcraft
Laurie Cabot, Power of the Witch
Scott Cunningham, Wicca: A Guide for the Solitary Practitioner
Gail Duff, The Wheel of the Wiccan Year
U. D Frater, Practical Sigil Magick
Marian Green, A Witch Alone
Elen Hawke, In the Circle: Crafting a Witches' Path
Lidia Pradas, The Complete Grimoire
Lidia Pradas, The Path of the Witch
Doreen Valiente, Where Witchcraft Lives

INDEX

Acknowledgments

I want to thank everyone who has been involved in making this book a reality. You have made my dream of becoming a published author come true. I'm truly grateful to everyone at Leaping Hare Press and for all their hard work, especially Chloe, Mel, and Lydia, as well as Viki who has brought my words to life with her beautiful artwork.

I would also like to thank my family and friends, especially mum and dad, my hubby, Rae, Viv, Len, Nana Mavis, and my sister Rachael. I am thankful beyond words for all your support, love, encouragement, and for always believing in me when I didn't believe in myself

I also want to thank the beautiful Witch of the Forest community on Instagram for always being a source of support and love, and for walking with me on my journey.